yOung
Exceptional
children

Monograph Series No. 1

Practical Ideas for Addressing Challenging Behaviors

**THE DIVISION FOR EARLY CHILDHOOD
OF THE COUNCIL FOR EXCEPTIONAL CHILDREN**

Susan Sandall and Michaelene Ostrosky
Co-Editors

Disclaimer

The opinions and information contained in the articles in this publication are those of the authors of the respective articles and not necessarily those of the co-editors of *Young Exceptional Children (YEC) Monograph Series* or of the Division for Early Childhood. Accordingly, the Division for Early Childhood assumes no liability or risk that may be incurred as a consequence, directly or indirectly, of the use and application of any of the contents of this publication.

The DEC does not perform due diligence on advertisers, exhibitors, or their products or services, and cannot endorse or guarantee that their offerings are suitable or accurate.

Published and Distributed by:

SOPRIS
WEST™
4093 Specialty Place • Longmont, CO 80504
(303) 651-2829 • FAX (303) 776-5934
www.sopriswest.com

27 Fort Missoula Road, Suite 2 • Missoula, MT 59804
(406) 543-0872 • FAX (406) 543-0877
www.dec-sped.org

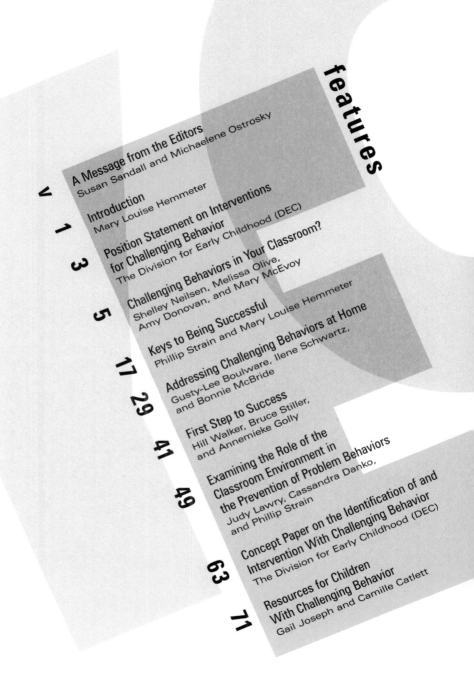

features

A Message from the Editors
Susan Sandall and Michaelene Ostrosky
v

Introduction
Mary Louise Hemmeter
1

Position Statement on Interventions for Challenging Behavior
The Division for Early Childhood (DEC)
3

Challenging Behaviors in Your Classroom?
Shelley Neilsen, Melissa Olive, Amy Donovan, and Mary McEvoy
5

Keys to Being Successful
Phillip Strain and Mary Louise Hemmeter
17

Addressing Challenging Behaviors at Home
Gusty-Lee Boulware, Ilene Schwartz, and Bonnie McBride
29

First Step to Success
Hill Walker, Bruce Stiller, and Annemieke Golly
41

Examining the Role of the Classroom Environment in the Prevention of Problem Behaviors
Judy Lawry, Cassandra Danko, and Phillip Strain
49

Concept Paper on the Identification of and Intervention With Challenging Behavior
The Division for Early Childhood (DEC)
63

Resources for Children With Challenging Behavior
Gail Joseph and Camille Catlett
71

A Message from the Editors

Welcome to the first issue of the *Young Exceptional Children* Monograph Series. DEC is pleased to introduce this new resource to DEC members as well as to other practitioners, families, and friends in the field of early intervention/early childhood special education.

The monograph series has two goals. First, it gathers together articles and resources on a highlighted topic of interest and need to the field. Second, it continues our effort, initiated in *Young Exceptional Children*, to translate research findings to effective and useful strategies for practitioners and families.

This monograph series represents an important step in DEC's efforts to increase our services to the field through products and publications. Through your responses to formal surveys as well as your informal feedback, we know that our DEC members and colleagues are eager for materials that they can use in their classrooms, programs, and homes. It is our intention that this monograph series will provide readers with just such useful materials. We hope that it will also serve a professional development function and a resource for courses, workshops, and similar activities.

Our aim is to publish the monograph series at least once each year. It will be closely linked with *Young Exceptional Children*. The topic will be identified by DEC members and the governance. Articles on that topic which have been previously published in *YEC* will be reviewed for possible inclusion in the monograph. The editors will also solicit additional articles from the field; these will undergo the usual peer review process. DEC position papers and concept papers will be included when appropriate to the topic. We will consider other formats for articles such as case studies or training activities. We welcome your ideas, encourage you to submit your work, and look forward to your feedback on the first issue in the monograph series.

We thank a number of individuals for their help in bringing the monograph to fruition. These people include the members of the Publications Committee; David Sexton, Mary Louise Hemmeter, Jerry Christensen, Barbara Smith, Linda Frederick, and the other members of the DEC governance and staff; and the *YEC* reviewers. Finally, we thank the authors of the articles in this issue. Your work on behalf of children and families is truly appreciated.

Co-Editors: Susan Sandall   Michaelene Ostrosky
               (206) 543-4011   (217) 333-0260
               ssandall@u.washington.edu   ostrosky@uiuc.edu

Introduction

Practical Ideas for Addressing Challenging Behaviors

Mary Louise Hemmeter, Ph.D., University of Kentucky

When DEC decided to publish a series of monographs, there was little debate about what the topic of the first issue should be. Several key factors contributed to the identification of this topic for the first monograph. In our roles as parents, teachers, trainers, consultants, and administrators, we are all acutely aware of the need for practical information on addressing children's challenging behaviors. The increase in the number of children who are at-risk or who have disabilities being served in inclusive settings has highlighted the need for practical strategies for dealing with the challenging behaviors of all children. Many teachers in these settings have had little or no training related to children with challenging behaviors. Year after year, at the DEC conference, sessions on challenging behaviors are consistently filled to capacity. Finally, as society struggles with more violent forms of challenging behaviors, we have become more aware of the need for intervening with challenging behaviors at an early age.

DEC began addressing this issue by developing a position statement on interventions for challenging behaviors. This position statement was initially developed in response to the growing trend in K-12 education toward removing children with behavior problems from the regular classroom. Fearing that this trend would filter down into the early childhood years, DEC wanted to be proactive in making the recommendation that most challenging behaviors, especially those exhibited by young children, can be addressed without removing the child from an inclusive setting. The position statement and subsequent concept paper are reprinted in this monograph and address three major points: (1) most challenging behaviors can be addressed through developmentally appropriate management techniques; (2) many effective preventative measures and intervention strategies are available for addressing challenging behaviors; and (3) families play a critical role in designing and carrying out interventions for challenging behaviors. The remaining articles in this monograph focus on the three key issues identified in the DEC position statement.

All of the articles in this monograph take a positive behavioral approach to addressing challenging behaviors that focuses on preventing challenging behaviors by evaluating the effects of the social and physical environment on children's behaviors, and teaching appropriate behaviors that serve the same function as challenging behaviors. Neilsen, Olive, Donovan, and McEvoy provide a foundation for understanding that challenging behaviors serve some communicative function for children and identifying that function and teaching appropriate behaviors are critical steps to addressing the challenging behavior. Strain and Hemmeter provide several suggestions for effectively dealing with challenging behaviors. These suggestions include not only evaluating the classroom environment but also the importance of adults evaluating their own attitudes toward children's challenging behaviors. Boulware, Schwartz, and McBride describe a five-step program for supporting families in dealing with their children's challenging behaviors. The steps in this program are based on the same concepts discussed throughout the articles in this monograph but with a focus on home environments and supporting families. Walker, Stiller, and Golly describe a specific home-school collaborative intervention designed for children who show early signs of an antisocial pattern of behavior. Each of the four articles described above provide background information, specific strategies for addressing challenging behaviors, and case studies or examples of how to implement the strategies. The final article, by Lawry, Danko, and Strain, uses a question and answer format to addresses common classroom issues and questions ("How can I make transition times less noisy and chaotic?").

Taken together, these articles provide information on preventing, identifying and addressing challenging behaviors in the classroom and at home. While these articles do not provide all of the information needed to deal with all challenging behaviors, they provide a framework and approach that can be used in a variety of situations. In addition, each article includes a list of references that provide more specific information.

THE DIVISION FOR EARLY CHILDHOOD

Division for Early Childhood (DEC) Position Statement on Interventions for Challenging Behavior

Adopted: April 1998

Many young children engage in challenging behavior in the course of early development. The majority of these children respond to developmentally appropriate management techniques.

Every parent, including parents of young children with disabilities, wants his or her child to attend schools, child care centers, or community-based programs that are nurturing and safe. Many young children engage in challenging behavior at various times during their early development. Typically, this behavior is short-term and decreases with age and use of appropriate guidance strategies. However, for some children these incidences of challenging behavior may become more consistent despite increased adult vigilance and use of appropriate guidance strategies. For these children, the challenging behavior may result in injury to themselves or others, cause damage to the physical environment, interfere with the acquisition of new skills, and/or socially isolate the child (Doss & Reichle, 1991). Additional intervention efforts may be required for these children.

DEC believes strongly that many types of services and intervention strategies are available to address challenging behavior.

Given the developmental nature of most challenging behavior, we believe there is a vast array of supplemental services that can be added to the home and education environment to increase the likelihood that children will learn appropriate behavior. A variety of intervention strategies can be implemented with either formal or informal support. Services and strategies could include, but are not limited to: (1) designing environments and activities to prevent challenging behavior and to help all children develop appropriate behavior; (2) utilizing effective behavioral interventions that are positive and address both form and function of a young child's challenging behavior; (3) adopting curricular modification and accommodation strategies designed to help young children learn behaviors appropriate to their settings; and (4) providing external consultation and technical assistance or additional staff support. In addition, all professionals who work with children in implementing IEPs or IFSPs must have opportunities to acquire knowledge and skills necessary for effective implementation of prevention and intervention programs.

> **DEC believes strongly that families play a critical role in designing and carrying out effective interventions for challenging behavior.**

Given the family-focused nature of early childhood education, we acknowledge the critical role that families play in addressing challenging behavior. Often challenging behavior occurs across places, people, and time, thus families are critical members of the intervention team. A coordinated effort between family members and professionals is needed to ensure interventions are effective and efficient and address both child and family needs and strengths. All decisions regarding the identification of a challenging behavior, possible interventions, placement, and ongoing evaluation must be made in accordance with the family through the IEP, IFSP, or other team decision-making processes.

Reference

Doss, L. S., & Reichle, J. (1991). Replacing excess behavior with an initial communicative repertoire. In J. Reichle, J. York, & J. Sigafoos (Eds.), *Implementing augmentative and alternative communication: Strategies for learners with severe disabilities*. Baltimore: Brookes.

Permission to copy not needed—distribution encouraged.

Challenging Behaviors in Your Classroom?

Don't React—Teach Instead!

Shelley L. Neilsen, M.Ed., University of Minnesota,
Melissa L. Olive, M.Ed., University of Nevada-Reno,
Amy Donovan, M.A., University of Minnesota, and
Mary McEvoy, Ph.D., University of Minnesota

We would like you to meet Tyler. He's the little guy who throws himself on the floor and screams, "No!" every time he is asked to do something. You probably know a child like Tyler because almost every preschool classroom has children with behaviors that are difficult to manage. Noncompliance, aggression, or self-injury can frustrate teachers and be problematic for children. Fortunately, there are strategies that can be implemented in many early childhood settings for assessing and managing these challenging behaviors. The purpose of this article is to discuss some of these strategies. In particular, we will focus on ways to assess challenging behaviors and describe how to use assessment information to design interventions that specifically target challenging behaviors.

While there are several ways to look at problem behaviors, we use a behavioral approach to discuss and analyze behavior and interventions. We recognize the behavioral approach is not the only approach, however it has demonstrated the most success in assessing and reducing challenging behaviors and increasing appropriate behaviors for a wide range of children with and without disabilities (Arndorfer, Miltenberger, Woster, Rortvedt, & Gaffaney, 1994; Dunlap et al., 1993; Kern, Childs, Dunlap, Clarke, & Falk, 1994; Scotti, Ujcich, Weigle, Holland, & Kirk, 1996; Strain et al., 1992; Umbreit & Blair, 1997). Consequently, many behavioral practices are considered best practice (Arndorfer & Miltenberger, 1993). For example, the recent reauthorization of IDEA recommends many of the procedures we discuss and specifically emphasizes functional behavioral assessment (Office of Special Education and Rehabilitation, 1997).

Throughout this article, certain behavioral terms such as "reinforcement" and "functional assessment of behavior" are used. While many of the terms are defined as they are discussed, there are a few terms we need to clarify up front. First, when we refer to "challenging behaviors" we mean behavior that is dangerous, disgusting, or disruptive (Risley, 1996). It is any action produced by a child that results in self-injury or injury to others, causes damage to the physical environment, interferes with learning new skills, and/or socially isolates the child (Doss & Reichle, 1991). Keeping this in mind, you can see that nearly all children occasionally engage in challenging behaviors whether they have a disability or not. Fortunately for most children, these behaviors occur infrequently; however, for some, challenging behaviors do occur frequently and with intensity.

Another frequently used term is "reinforcer." Basically, a reinforcer is anything that occurs following a behavior that increases or maintains the likelihood of the behavior occurring again in the future (Alberto & Troutman, 1995). For many children reinforcers include hugs, smiles, praise, toys, and food. Other children are reinforced by any sort of attention (including negative) or by avoiding activities and adults. Often, children engage in challenging behaviors to obtain some sort of reinforcer (e.g., attention).

In the past we tended to use "cookbook" approaches to alter challenging behaviors. If Tina spit, we implemented an intervention designed to decrease spitting; if Joey bit, we turned to an intervention to decrease biting. As teachers, we were attending to the "form" of the challenging behavior (e.g., kicking, biting, etc.). This approach works for some children some of the time but often is ineffective. Through nearly 30 years of research, we've learned that behavior serves a specific function or purpose and is predicted by the events that take place before (i.e., antecedents) and maintained by events that take place after (i.e., consequences) the behavior occurs (Bijou, Peterson, & Ault, 1968; O'Neill, Horner, Albin, Storey, & Sprague, 1990; Reichle & Wacker, 1993).

When designing effective interventions, it is critical to consider both the form and function of the behavior (Reichle & Wacker, 1993). While the form of the behavior can be anything from yelling, to biting, to breaking toys, the function of a challenging behavior typically falls under one of two general areas: obtaining an outcome (i.e., positive reinforcement) or getting out of or avoiding an outcome (i.e., negative reinforcement) (see Figure 1).

Although behavior is rather complex and does not occur in a vacuum, this next example simply illustrates how adults engage in a behavior to

Figure 1: Function of Challenging Behaviors

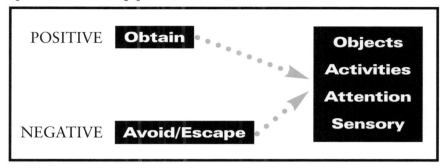

obtain an outcome. Think about a typical exchange with a vending machine. We put money in vending machines (form) to obtain a snack (function). In this example, the function of our behavior is to obtain an item. Now examine a classroom example. Bailey, a child with Down Syndrome, often pulls her teacher's hair. Each time she does this, the teacher becomes very excited and tells her to "Stop!" In this example, the function of Bailey's behavior might be to obtain the teacher's attention. To Bailey, attention may act as a reinforcer. By pulling hair (form), she receives attention (function) and learns that she can consistently and independently obtain the teacher's attention every time she pulls her hair.

Let's think about an example of behavior that serves a function to avoid an activity. Unlike Bailey's attention-seeking behavior with her teacher, at lunch she engages in a challenging behavior to avoid attention. She pushes the trays (form) of all the children who sit around her until everyone leaves to sit at other tables (function). Bailey does not like to sit with others at lunch and she avoids this situation by engaging in a behavior that results in everyone leaving her alone.

Another common example of avoiding occurs during "circle time." Abby, a child diagnosed with autism, bites (form) Ben during circle time and is sent away from the group (function). You notice a pattern emerging: Abby comes to circle, she bites, and you send her out of the circle. It appears you are implementing an intervention to decrease her biting, however, removing her from the circle may be reinforcing because the requirements of circle time are removed every time she bites.

In the example with Bailey, she used two different forms of challenging behaviors (i.e., pulling hair and pushing trays) for two different functions (for attention and to avoid). However, it is possible for a single form of a behavior to serve more than one function. Remember Tyler, the boy described at the beginning of this article who tantrummed when asked to follow directions? He also tantrummed when his toys were taken away, when his mom was talking to the teacher, and when he did not get his favorite cup at snack. In this way, the same form (tantrumming) served many functions: getting out of following directions, getting toys back, and securing his mother's attention.

In a similar manner, several forms of behavior may serve one function. Consider Tina, who spits. She also kicks, bites, scratches, and pinches, all, we think, for a teacher's attention. She uses many different forms of behavior, all of which could serve a similar function (see Figure 2).

In deciding how to change Tina's behavior, the first step is to determine the function of that behavior. We do this by using a process called functional assessment (O'Neill et al., 1990). Functional assessment allows us to look closely at the events that happen immediately before and after challenging behaviors. This helps identify people, events, or activities that may trigger challenging behaviors and to make predictions about when those behaviors are likely to occur (Strain et al., 1992). The components of functional assessment include interviews, direct observations, and environmental manipulations.

The interview process is an important first step in understanding the function of challenging behavior. Interviews with a parent, teacher, or child care provider can contribute valuable assessment information. These can be informal, such as simply asking questions: "When Mary starts to cry, are you interacting with other children?" or "What kinds of requests are you making of Michael when he throws toys?" You could

Figure 2: Examples of Challenging Behaviors and Their Possible Functions

Form	Possible Functions
Crying	To obtain attention
Crying	To get out of or avoid a specific activity
Crying	To indicate pain in ear
Throwing objects	To indicate anger, frustration
Throwing objects	To listen to the sound it makes
Hitting self	To obtain attention
Hitting self	To get out of or avoid requests
Hitting self	To gain endorphin release

also ask questions about what happens following the behavior, such as: "What happens after Jamie bites a peer?" or "What do you do after Demario climbs the entertainment center?"

Another type of interview is more formal and structured. O'Neill and colleagues (1990) developed an interview guide that provides questions about antecedents and consequences related to problem behaviors. This in-depth interview solicits information about when the behavior occurs, what interventions have been tried, the effectiveness of previous interventions, the child's preferences, and medical or physiological conditions. Rating scales can also be informative. One popular scale is the "Motivational Assessment Scale" (Durand & Crimmins, 1990), a 16-item, empirically-validated rating scale used to assess the possible function of challenging behaviors. This scale is particularly useful because it is fast, easy to use, and can be completed by anyone involved in the child's life.

The next step, direct observation, provides critical, first-hand information about the possible functions of a child's challenging behavior. A popular method of direct observation is the "ABC analysis" (Bijou, Peterson, & Ault, 1968). "ABC" is an acronym for antecedent, behavior, and consequence; in using this analysis we document each of these three components. The antecedent is what occurs immediately before a challenging behavior. Some examples of common antecedents that might trigger challenging behaviors are teacher directions, absence of teacher attention, difficult activities, and transition times. The behavior is the form of the behavior (e.g., hitting, crying, biting, running away, etc.). It is very important to clearly identify the form of a challenging behavior. If the description of the behavior of interest is too broad, pinpointing the function of the behavior may be difficult.

For example, Bobby may scream to obtain a teacher's attention and throw toys to escape clean-up time. Both behaviors could be considered a tantrum, but if the teacher records each of these as tantrums, the function of each behavior could be unclear since each serves a different function. What happens immediately following the behavior is the consequence. Typical consequences of behavior include: obtaining adult attention (e.g., redirection and verbal reprimand), receiving a favorite toy, or avoiding an undesirable activity such as picking up toys (e.g., through time-out).

There are numerous ways to use an ABC analysis in classrooms. The most common is a narrative recording which consists of documenting the antecedents, behaviors, and consequences. For an example of this type of ABC analysis, see Figure 3. Whether using this type of narrative version or a different version such as that recommended by O'Neill et al. (1990), the important component of an ABC analysis is to try to find a link between the behavior and its antecedents and consequences.

While interviews and direct observation methods are necessary in the beginning in order to understand the function of challenging behaviors, an environmental manipulation may be necessary to truly verify the function of the behavior. In an environmental manipulation, specific antecedents and/or consequences are altered to see how these alternatives affect challenging behaviors (e.g., When the teacher provides attention throughout free play is there a decrease in challenging behaviors?). The scope of this article does not allow us to discuss environmental manipulation in detail. However, if you are interested in learning more

Figure 3: ABC Analysis for Tyler

Date & Time	Antecedent	Behavior	Consequence	Perceived Function/ Comments
	What happened before?	What did the child do?	What happened after?	What was the possible function of the behavior?
1/10 10:30	3 minutes of art activity have passed, Tyler is not participating. The teacher asks Tyler to paint the picture.	Tyler screams, "No," and throws his paper on the floor.	The teacher walks away. Tyler leaves the art table and goes to the block area to play.	Get out of art activity
1/10 11:30	The teacher announces that it's time to get ready for lunch and takes Tyler's hand to guide him to the sink to wash his hands.	Tyler falls to the floor and starts crying.	The teacher says, "Okay, Tyler, you don't have to wash your hands, but you have to use a handi-wipe."	Avoid washing hands? Or does he just like the handi-wipes?
1/11 8:30	The teacher tells the children it's time to clean up and go to circle. The teacher walks toward Tyler.	Tyler throws a truck and screams, "No, I don't want to clean up."	The teacher says, "Tyler, no throwing toys. Go to time-out." Tyler sits in a chair while the rest of the children clean up. When clean-up is over, Tyler goes to the circle with the rest of the children.	Avoid clean-up

about these procedures refer to O'Neill et al. (1990) for a complete description of how to conduct an in-depth analysis of the function of a challenging behavior.

Assessing the function of a child's behavior is a critical step in managing that behavior, but it is only the beginning. Reactions to the behavior and the antecedents that set the stage for the behavior still must be modified. Why is our reaction so important? Because more often than not, our reaction serves to maintain and even increase the challenging behavior. For example, what if Jeremiah, a child with attention deficit disorder (ADD), had just thrown his art materials on the floor, screamed, and pulled Ellen's hair. What would you do in this situation? When challenging behaviors occur in the classroom, our first response is usually emotional; we tend to reprimand, lecture, or single out the child for engaging in negative behaviors. Our intention is to help Jeremiah understand why the behavior is wrong. We might first tell him it's not okay to hurt our friends. Then we may point out that Ellen is crying and encourage Jeremiah to tell us why he pulled her hair. We also might sit with Jeremiah until he picks up the materials he threw and/or apologizes to Ellen. Although out intentions are good, they are often unnecessary. Most children learn quickly which behaviors are inappropriate and which ones will earn an immediate and emotional response. When a child's goal is to obtain one-to-one teacher time, he or she can do so quickly by engaging in such challenging behaviors.

Another typical response to challenging behaviors that may unintentionally serve to increase the behaviors is to remove the child from an area or to remove instructional materials. Imagine that Jeremiah is not trying to get the teacher's attention, but rather he is trying to avoid the art activity. He may have reached a point in the activity that is difficult, or he may dislike art. If our response to the behavior is to remove Jeremiah from the area, he has achieved his goal. If we remove the materials that were thrown, we still may be responding in a way that increases the behavior. If those were the materials that made the art difficult, then without them, the activity is no longer problematic for Jeremiah. If your response is more similar to the first one we discussed, and you would spend several minutes talking to him about why that behavior is not okay, Jeremiah would still successfully avoid the activity, if only for a few minutes.

Often children engage in challenging behaviors because this has been the most effective way to get attention or avoid activities. In a way, the children in our examples are using their challenging behaviors to communicate. Instead of reacting to the challenging behaviors, we should focus on teaching the children a more appropriate way to obtain attention or cope with an unpleasant activity. One way to do this is to consistently respond to a positive behavior (often one we teach the child to use) and not react to a challenging behavior. The goal is for the child to use the appropriate behavior, rather than the challenging behavior.

There are many responses we can teach children to use instead of engaging in challenging behaviors. We can teach them to say, through spoken language, gestures, or graphic symbols: "I want you to play with me," "I want my favorite toy," "I want a break," "I'm all done," " No, I don't like that," or "I need some help." (see Figure 4) Replacing challenging behaviors with a form of communication is called functional communication training (FCT) (Carr et al., 1994). Functional communication training teaches children another way to obtain the same outcome they obtained when they engaged in challenging behaviors. For example, if we know Tina is using challenging behaviors to get attention, we could teach her to ask for attention in an appropriate way, making it unnecessary for her to engage in challenging behaviors to receive the attention.

Let's plan a communication intervention for Molly, a child who starts throwing toys every time the teacher announces "clean-up time." Previously, time-out was used as a consequence to throwing toys. However, if the function of the behavior is to avoid clean-up time, then we were probably inadvertently reinforcing Molly's behavior. Now assume that we assessed the function of the behavior and the results indicated that Molly engaged in this challenging behavior to avoid clean-up. We could then teach her to say, "Please help." In this case, Molly's challenging behavior (i.e., throwing toys) and the appropriate behavior (i.e., saying, "Please help.") serve the same purpose; both responses get Molly out of clean-up.

Figure 4: Communicative Replacement Options

Possible Function of a Challenging Behavior	Communicative Replacement	Verbal Response	Gestural Response	Symbol Selection
Attention	Request attention	Say, "Play please."	Sign "play"	Touch symbol "toys"
Attention or avoidance	Request assistance or request a work check	Say, "Help please." Say, "Is this work right?"	Sign "help" Sign "look"	Touch symbol "help" or "work check"
Avoidance	Request a break Reject an item	Say, "I'm done now." Say, "No thanks."	Sign "finished" Sign "no"	Touch symbol "break" or "no"

For this intervention to work, the appropriate behavior (i.e., communication) must provide the exact outcome that the challenging behavior previously provided. Equally important, the challenging behavior should no longer be effective in providing that same outcome. When Molly says, "Please help," she is assisted with clean-up. Now when she throws toys, she does *not* get out of clean-up. You might be saying to yourself, "But then Molly doesn't have to pick up toys independently." You're right; for the time being, she is allowed to avoid picking up all her toys. Remember, though, she was not cleaning up any toys when she was in time-out. With this intervention, first we decrease the challenging behavior and teach her an appropriate way to get out of the activity, then we can begin to work on ways to encourage Molly to pick up her toys. It will be a lot easier to teach Molly to pick up toys when she is not throwing them around the room.

Functional communication training is an "antecedent intervention." This means it is implemented before any challenging behavior occurs. Antecedent interventions prevent the teacher and child from having to deal with challenging behaviors (Carr et al., 1994). To use antecedent interventions, we must know when the challenging behavior typically occurs and intervene before the child reaches this point. Take Molly, for example. We know that she engages in a challenging behavior when she is asked to clean up. Instead of simply giving the clean-up instruction and waiting for Molly to engage in the challenging behavior, we teach her to ask for help before the clean-up instruction is given. When clean-up time is approaching, we tell Molly, "It's almost time to clean up; say, 'Help, please'." This way, Molly requests assistance before she is expected to clean up; therefore she never needs to engage in the challenging behavior because we help her with clean-up when she asks appropriately.

Let's think about what would happen if we implemented the same intervention after the challenging behavior occurred. We give the instruction to clean up, and Molly starts throwing toys. We then approach Molly and say, "Say 'Help please'." In this example two critical mistakes are made. First, the intervention is implemented *following* the challenging behavior. By teaching Molly to ask for help after she has engaged in the challenging behavior, we may inadvertently be teaching Molly to engage in the challenging behavior first and then request help. Second, implementing the intervention following a challenging behavior requires a response to the behavior every time the teacher announces that it is clean-up time. This creates more work for the teachers because they are forced to deal repeatedly with Molly's challenging behavior. On the other hand, when we teach the new behavior in the absence of the challenging behavior or before it occurs, we prevent the challenging behavior from ever occurring and we don't run the risk of teaching the child an inappropriate sequence of behaviors (e.g., throwing toys and then saying, "Help please.").

Let's return to Tyler, the little boy in the first example. We completed a functional assessment on his challenging behavior (see Figure 3). Remember, he threw himself on the floor and screamed every time he was asked to do something. The results of the functional assessment indicated his challenging behavior resulted in avoiding a variety of activities, such as clean-up, snack preparation, and table-top activities. Therefore, the teachers concluded that the function of his challenging behavior was

to avoid these activities. Based on this information, the teachers decided to teach the appropriate communicative behavior, "I'm all done." When it was time for clean-up, Tyler was prompted to say, "I'm all done," and the teachers would give him a short break from clean-up time. This eliminated his need to tantrum to avoid the task and taught him a more appropriate way to express himself.

For those of us who work with children like Tyler, challenging behavior is part of everyday life. We are constantly evaluating and reevaluating the way we handle such behavior. Functional assessment provides us with a tool for determining the events, activities, or people that maintain a child's behavior so we can avoid the frustration of a series of failed interventions. When we know the function of a behavior, we know where to focus our intervention efforts. Similarly, reacting repeatedly to the same behaviors without seeing any behavior reduction is both tiring and frustrating. This article offers suggestions for how to plan for, rather than react to, challenging behaviors. The combination of functional assessment and functional communication training (i.e., teaching a more appropriate behavior to replace a challenging behavior) is a powerful intervention package that can be used in any classroom for children with and without disabilities. It does require that we change the way we react to aggressive and disruptive behavior; but it also allows us to spend much more time teaching. The result is well worth the effort.

Note
This work was supported in part by Grant No. HO29D050063, Preparation of Leadership Personnel: Training Leadership Personnel to Address the Needs of Preschoolers Who Engage in Challenging Behavior, U.S. Department of Education awarded to Joe Reichle, Ph.D., and Mary McEvoy, Ph.D. at the University of Minnesota.

References
Alberto, P., & Troutman, A. (1995). *Applied behavior analysis for teachers.* Englewood Cliffs, NJ: Prentice Hall.

Arndorfer, R., & Miltenberger, R. (1993). Functional assessment and treatment of challenging behavior: A review with implications for early childhood. *Topics in Early Childhood Special Education, 13*(1), 82-105.

Arndorfer, R., Miltenberger, R., Woster, S., Rortvedt, A., & Gaffaney, T. (1994). Home-based descriptive and experimental analysis of problem behaviors in children. *Topics in Early Childhood Special Education, 14*(1), 64-87.

Bijou, S. W., Peterson, R. F., & Ault, M. H. (1968). A method to integrate descriptive and experimental field studies at the level of data and empirical concepts. *Journal of Applied Behavior Analysis, 1,* 175-191.

Carr, E. G., Levin, L., McConnachie, G., Carlson, J., Kemp, D., & Smith, C. (1994). *Communication-based intervention for problem behavior: A user's guide for producing positive change.* Baltimore: Paul H. Brookes.

Doss, L., & Reichle, J. (1991). Replacing excess behavior with an initial communicative repertoire. In J. Reichle, J. York, & J. Sigafoos (Eds.), *Implementing augmentative and alternative communication: Strategies for learners with severe disabilities.* Baltimore: Paul H. Brookes.

Dunlap, G., Kern, L., dePerczel, M., Clarke, S., Wilson, D., Childs, K., White, R., & Falk, G. (1993). Functional analysis of classroom variables for students with emotional and behavioral disorders. *Behavioral Disorders, 18*(4), 275-291.

Durand, V. M., & Crimmins, D. B. (1990). Assessment. In V.M. Durand (Ed.), *Severe behavior problems: A functional communication training approach* (pp. 31-82). New York: Guilford.

Kern, L., Childs, K., Dunlap, G., Clarke, S., & Falk, G. (1994). Using assessment-based curricular intervention to improve the classroom behavior of a student with emotional and behavioral challenges. *Journal of Applied Behavior Analysis, 27,* 7-19.

Office of Special Education and Rehabilitation. (1997, May). IDEA, 1997 general information home page [On-line]. Available: www.edgov/offices/OSERS/IDEA/summary.html.

O'Neill, R. E., Horner, R. H., Albin, R., Storey, K., & Sprague, J. (1990). *Functional assessment of problem behavior: A practical assessment guide.* Pacific Grove, CA: Brookes/Cole.

Reichle, J., & Wacker, D. (1993). *Communicative alternatives to challenging behavior: Integrating functional assessment and intervention strategies.* Baltimore: Paul H. Brookes.

Risley, T. (1996). Get a life! Positive behavioral intervention for challenging behavior through life arrangement and life coaching. In L.K. Koegel, R.L. Koegel, & G. Dunlap (Eds.), *Positive behavioral support: Including people with difficult behavior in the community* (pp. 425-437). Baltimore: Paul H. Brookes.

Scotti, J., Ujcich, J., Weigle, K., Holland, C., & Kirk, K. (1996). Interventions with challenging behavior of persons with developmental disabilities: A review of current research practices. *Journal for the Association for Persons with Severe Handicaps, 21*(3), 123-134.

Strain, P., McConnell, S., Carta, J., Fowler, S., Neisworth, J., & Wolery, M. (1992). Behaviorism in early intervention. *Topics in Early Childhood Special Education, 12*(1), 121-141.

Umbreit, J., & Blair, K. (1997). Using structural analysis to facilitate treatment of aggression and noncompliance in a young child at risk for behavioral disorders. *Behavioral Disorders, 22*(2), 75-86.

Keys to Being Successful
When Confronted With Challenging Behaviors

Phillip S. Strain, Ph.D., University of Colorado at Denver, and **Mary Louise Hemmeter, Ph.D.**, University of Kentucky

Let us begin with a definition of challenging behaviors. The temptation is to simply list various actions such as screaming, hitting others, running away, cursing, etc. The problem with this approach is the potential list is endless; and, it would be unlikely any two people would agree on the list content. Herein lies our first and perhaps the most critical key to success.

key 1: We each define challenging behaviors based upon our unique set of past experiences, values, instructional practices, and institutional guidelines.

Because we each define challenging behaviors in our unique, idiosyncratic ways, we are part and parcel of the problem! Some of us have a very low threshold, becoming upset when children are "fidgety" at circle time. Others see no cause for concern, much less for systematic intervention, in this situation. The hard truth is that the most accurate, useful definition for challenging behavior is this: Challenging behavior is any behavior that is disturbing to you and that you wish to see stopped.

By understanding our unique contribution to the definition of challenging behavior we can then move ahead to the second key to success.

key 2: We each must become more "comfortable" with challenging behaviors if we are to be successful agents of change.

By "comfortable" we do not mean that one should work to like obnoxious behaviors or simply not pay attention to them. However, if we know and accept the fact that certain child behaviors are disturbing to us (by definition), we must also be willing to acknowledge the inevitable human condition of being less than our best when we are under stress: in this case, stress caused by child behaviors that can result in our being flooded with feelings of anger, frustration, embarrassment, and even hopelessness. How do we get more comfortable?

The answer is simple, but often difficult in practice. We suggest the following:
1. Learn to recognize those situations that are disturbing;
2. Share those feelings and situations with colleagues or other adults;
3. Develop mutual support systems among colleagues or other adults; and
4. Strive to expand your alternatives to prevent or intervene with those disturbing situations.

As we work to become more comfortable with disturbing behaviors we will know our efforts are successful when we:
1. Stop thinking about "removing the child" as the "real" answer to our problem.
2. Stop blaming disturbing behaviors on uncontrollable, extraneous events (e.g., "He just comes to school in these moods," "If only her family cared more," "If he doesn't get his pill on time, this is what happens.").
3. Start celebrating where we are now in comparison to where we were.
4. Start to become a resource to our colleagues and friends who are struggling with their own unique challenging situations.

The final step in becoming more comfortable with challenging behaviors involves altering certain ideas and expectations most of us have regarding the effectiveness of interventions to prevent or remediate challenging events.

What are these "misguided" ideas and expectations? While many of us know better at an intellectual level, we often launch our interventions with the expectations of "never ever" and "fixed for good." These are totally understandable; no one desires to be cursed at or spat upon "just occasionally"! Yet, the expectations of "never ever" and "fixed for good" are a no win set-up for children and those striving to help. If we fail to see, acknowledge, and celebrate the success of moving from 15 spats per day to twice per week, for example, because "never ever" is the only acceptable outcome, then we become the eternal victims of our emotional response to disturbing behaviors. We may, indeed we should, work toward moving from twice per week to fewer and fewer episodes. The real challenge is to be sufficiently comfortable enough to recognize the mutual success that we and the children have achieved along the way.

Closely linked to the dangerous expectations of "never ever" and "fixed for good" is the idea or perhaps just the hope that things will get better, not worse, once we begin some systematic intervention. Regrettably, the reality is often just the opposite.

Especially in cases of long-standing behavior problems, children often meet our initial intervention attempts by escalating the frequency and/or amplitude (e.g., screaming louder) of their challenging behaviors. Our challenge is to remain persistent and steadfast, with the correct expectation that things often get worse before they get better.

A third misguided expectation is that our *initial attempts* at designing some intervention to prevent or remediate challenging behaviors will have a high probability of ultimate success. We think the reality is closer to 30%. Even with relatively unlimited resources and intervention planners with decades of experience, initial designs most often need to be changed. Our challenge, given this initial success ratio, is to:

1. Be humble in presenting our initial ideas to colleagues and consumers.
2. Set into place a careful system for monitoring intervention effects.
3. Meet regularly (at least every two weeks) as a team to discuss the need to modify the intervention.

As we begin to design preventive and/or remedial interventions (hopefully with a clear and accurate understanding of our own role in defining challenging behaviors and in judging their probable outcome), our next key to success is as follows:

key 3: Any challenging behavior that persists over time is "working" for the child.

Key 3 highlights the importance of our understanding the causes of challenging behaviors. They do not just spontaneously erupt (although it may feel that way). They are not simply a behavioral characteristic of certain groups of children. Nor are they accurately viewed as some out-of-control, bizarre, nonfunctional child behaviors. Rather, we have come to understand that most of these challenging behaviors have a purposeful, communicative function. However effective or ineffective, these behaviors represent the child's attempts to communicate a variety of different messages, including:

1. You're asking me to do something that is too difficult.
2. I don't understand what you want.
3. I want a certain thing, and I want it now.
4. I'm bored, pay some attention to me.

Knowing that challenging behaviors are designed in most cases to express some desire or preference changes the intervention equation

180°. It is no longer legitimate or professionally acceptable to simply work toward making children stop doing a certain behavior; instead, we need to focus on teaching the child new, easy, and more socially acceptable ways to communicate.

Our fourth key to success builds directly on the third. Let us examine more closely the communication examples mentioned above. They each communicate a desire or want that could, potentially, have been *anticipated* and in so doing, the challenging behavior could have been prevented.

For example, providing activities closer to the child's developmental capability, being more concrete in making a request (e.g., showing a picture along with asking), using highly desirable toys and materials to teach many different skills, and providing a rich array of positive feedback to children could, in order, well be the precise preventive intervention needed to address each of the aforementioned "communications." Herein lies of fourth key.

key 4: When prevention becomes the goal, as it should, the focus of intervention planning changes from what we might do to the child to what we might change about our own classroom practices.

Evaluating and changing classroom practices as a strategy for dealing with challenging behaviors has the benefit of not only addressing the behavior of the child or children in question but also reduces the likelihood that other children will exhibit challenging behaviors. While changes in the following practices may not reduce or prevent all challenging behaviors, these changes are easier to implement than more systematic behavior change programs.

In the following section we will describe four categories of preventive practices that should be evaluated: (1) physical environment; (2) activities and materials; (3) scheduling; and (4) strategies for promoting appropriate behaviors. The focus of this discussion is on changes to the classroom or home environment for the purpose of increasing children's appropriate engagement while preventing or decreasing the likelihood of challenging behaviors.

Physical Environment

There are several factors related to the physical environment that can affect children's behavior. These things may be easier to change than any of the other practices discussed in this article. First, the arrangement of learning centers should be considered. Centers that have minimal space, or centers that are associated with different activity levels and/or noise levels (e.g., blocks and listening centers) and are in close proximity to one another may result in conflicts between children as well as other behaviors that may be considered by teachers to be problematic (e.g., disturbing your neighbor).

Second, traffic patterns in classrooms are often problematic. Classrooms arranged such that there are wide open spaces in the middle of the room may serve the function of encouraging children to run from one activity to another. Classrooms that are overly crowded with minimal room for moving from one center to another may result in behaviors such as bumping into one another, knocking things off of shelves, or knocking chairs over. In order to prevent these types of problems, the following things should be considered:

- Are there boundaries between centers that delineate the centers but which are open enough to provide adequate space for multiple children to be in each center at the same time?
- Are centers arranged such that noisy centers (e.g., blocks, dramatic play) are located some distance from quieter centers (e.g., listening, books)?
- Are centers located in close proximity to the materials and equipment needed for each center? For example, is the art area located near a sink?
- Are the centers arranged such that there is adequate space to allow for easy movement between centers (including movement of wheelchairs) while ensuring there are not wide open spaces in which children are likely to run?

Activities and Materials

One key to preventing challenging behaviors is ensuring children are actively and appropriately engaged in activities with materials or people. Engagement refers to the amount of time children spend interacting appropriately with their environment (McWilliam, 1991). When children are engaged with people or materials, they are less likely to exhibit challenging behaviors. There are several things we can do to support children's engagement with their environment. First, and perhaps most important, we must provide children with interesting materials and activities. While this may seem obvious in theory, it is not always as easy in practice. Given that children have different interests, there must be a variety of materials and activities from which children can choose. In addition, there must be an adequate number of materials in order to reduce the likelihood that children will argue over materials.

Second, we must ensure there are materials appropriate to the developmental levels of all children in the classroom. Activities or materials that are too difficult or not challenging enough may cause children to be frustrated, and frustration often leads to behaviors that many would consider challenging.

Third, even when we provide a variety of materials in terms of both type and difficulty level, we cannot assume all children will engage with those materials or activities independently. Some children (e.g., those with more severe disabilities) will need support from adults and/or peers in terms of choosing an activity as well as participating in the activity once they have selected it. Other children may need ongoing positive feedback from adults and/or peers in order to maintain their engagement with a material or activity and to prevent them from wandering around the room during free choice time.

Scheduling

A classroom schedule that is well-designed and is implemented consistently may be the single most important factor in preventing challenging behaviors. There are two key issues which should be considered related to scheduling. First, routines are critical to supporting young children's appropriate behaviors. There should be a routine schedule that is followed on a daily basis, and the children must be aware of that schedule. Schedules that change from day to day and week to week prevent children from learning routines. When children know what to do and when to do it, they are less likely to exhibit behaviors that might be viewed as challenging. Of course, routine does not imply sameness, merely predictability regarding the *type* of activity that comes next.

The second issue related to scheduling has to do with transitions. Too many transitions, too little structure during transitions, transitions that are too long, or transitions that occur without any warning set the stage for challenging behaviors. One of the problems with transitions is they are often characterized by children waiting for extended periods of time with nothing to do while they are waiting. Challenging behaviors are likely to occur when children have nothing to do (i.e., when they are not engaged). Consider the following suggestions for structuring transitions to reduce the likelihood of challenging behaviors:

- Minimize the number of daily transitions, especially those that require children to move between activities as a large group. Large group transitions are likely to result in waiting time for some children. Allowing children to move to a new activity as they complete a prior one will ensure that children do not spend time waiting on others to complete the activity.
- When possible, structure transitions such that one adult reads a story, sings songs, or does some other activity for those children who complete the transition most quickly, while another adult assists the other children in making the transition. This will provide the children who transition quickly with something to do while they are waiting and if the activity is interesting, it may reduce the time it takes other children to transition.
- Provide children with a warning shortly before a transition is going to take place. This gives children an opportunity to finish what they are doing prior to having to put it away. This warning can be made by ringing a bell, blinking the lights, singing a clean-up song, or providing a verbal instruction to the children. Remember that different children may need different types of warnings (e.g., verbal, auditory, pictures) either because of sensory impairments or other learning characteristics.

Promoting Appropriate Behaviors

As teachers, we often assume children will learn appropriate social skills naturally through interactions with children and adults. Rather than focusing on teaching appropriate social behaviors, we focus on what to do when children "misbehave." We would like to suggest that preventing challenging behaviors depends upon the extent to which we teach appropriate behaviors. For example, we should not expect children to follow the rules if they have not been provided with instructions to do so. We might assume that kindergarten age children know about the importance of sharing. However, children who are in school for the first time may have had limited experiences with sharing their toys. It is not fair to discipline them for not sharing when they have not been taught about the importance of sharing.

So, what can we do to teach appropriate behaviors to children? First, we should establish a few important class rules and ensure all the children understand the rules. One way to increase the likelihood that children will understand the rules is to include them in making the rules. Once the rules are established, they can be posted in the room using signs that have both words and pictures. In order for children to understand and follow the rules, it will be important to discuss the rules on a regular basis and to talk about why the rules are important. In addition, children will need to see that the rules have consistent consequences.

Second, as adults, we should model appropriate social behaviors in the classroom. If we expect children not to yell when they are mad, we should model appropriate ways of expressing our anger. We should not expect children not to yell when they have observed the teacher yelling. Strategies for modeling appropriate social behaviors should be planned and implemented as appropriate opportunities arise.

Third, we can teach appropriate social behaviors by commenting on children who are exhibiting appropriate behaviors (e.g., "Jesse, thank you for helping Sarah put up her toys"), role-playing examples of appropriate social behaviors (e.g., role-playing what children might do if someone takes something away from them), and talking about social behaviors during group times (e.g., "I saw some people sharing their toys during center time. Can anyone tell me about someone they saw today who was sharing?"). By teaching appropriate social behaviors, we provide children with options for how they might respond to problematic situations. As we discussed earlier, children often exhibit challenging behaviors because they don't know any other way to respond to a situation.

When Prevention Methods Fail

When evaluating our classroom practices, we must keep in mind that the goal of this exercise is to determine how we can change our environment and practices to increase the likelihood that children will engage with materials, activities, and people as a strategy for decreasing the likelihood that children will engage in challenging behaviors. Changes in the physical environment, the schedule, the activities, and the social context of the classroom should be made with the goal of increasing engagement.

We have offered four keys we think are critical to being successful when dealing with challenging behaviors. While we believe attention to these issues will assist in reducing challenging behaviors, we are not suggesting these tactics are adequate for addressing all problem behaviors. The focus of our discussion has been on what we, as teachers, can do to change our attitudes about challenging behaviors, to reduce the likelihood of challenging behaviors occurring, and to deal with challenging behaviors using a more positive approach that considers the context and function of the child's behavior. We recognize that even when we have addressed these issues in our classrooms, there will be occasions of challenging behaviors.

Because of the seriousness of some challenging behaviors (e.g., biting, poking other children with scissors), and their persistence in the face of preventive measures, a more direct, labor-intensive approach may be needed. How do we decide when our preventive efforts are truly overmatched? How do we decide to call in outside help? While we have no easy answers, we can suggest that the team involved with the child spend the necessary time to ask and answer the questions on the question checklist provided in Table 1 (see following page) prior to implementing any more elaborate strategies than those we have offered.

Concluding Thoughts

A mutual colleague of ours is fond of saying, "You can't provide any service if nobody comes." It is a seemingly self-evident, almost trite comment. Yet, when it comes to young children with challenging behaviors, it nicely summarizes the most fundamental of issues. For many children who engage in challenging behaviors, the greatest programmatic efforts are often devoted to *removing* these children from the setting. We sincerely hope this paper will inspire more mature, sophisticated, and accepting responses to challenging behaviors.

The status quo alternative of "antiseptic bouncing" simply does not address the problem.

Table 1: Questions to Ask and Answer Prior to Implementing Interventions

CHECKLIST

Question 1

Are there any historical or contemporary events in the child's life that may help us better understand the behavior in question? This is the "big picture" question that one must never ignore, since an unknown fraction of challenging behaviors in classroom settings have their origin *outside* this environment. Examples of events that we know can impact the onset and increase of challenging behaviors include: (1) observing or being the victim of abuse and violence, (2) prolonged separations from primary caregivers, (3) poor nutrition and health care, and (4) unpredictable, punitive discipline practices.

Question 2

Are we convinced that the intended goal is developmentally appropriate, functional, and clearly related to an improved quality of life for the child? This very demanding question asks all members of the team to examine their individual definitions of challenging behaviors. In some cases, all team members may agree that a change in the challenging behavior(s) satisfies this question. For example, if the challenging behavior is running into the street, few would argue that staying on the sidewalk would not be appropriate, functional, and directly related to an improved quality of life for a four-year old. If the behavior considered to be challenging, however, is leaving circle time after 20 minutes, disagreement may well occur on the team. Our suggestion is to not proceed with a more intensive intervention if this question cannot be unanimously answered in the affirmative.

Question 3

Have we put into place all necessary components of the environment (e.g., an enriched setting, developmentally and individually appropriate materials, reasonable behavior/activity choices, a clear schedule of activities, strategies to minimize transition difficulties) that may prevent challenging behaviors? The purpose of question 3 is to ensure you are working smarter, not merely harder, to address challenging behaviors. The preventive interventions we have recommended are highly time- and cost-efficient, and should be given a fair trial before proceeding to intervention alternatives that likely demand a reorganization or the addition of staff resources.

Question 4

Do primary caregivers value the goals of the planned intervention and do they endorse the use of its specific strategies? While it is most advantageous to create systems of behavioral support for children's challenging behaviors that represent close harmony in tactics used across school and home settings, it is *absolutely* imperative that values and practices are not at odds. This question should force the team to solicit, at a minimum, the primary caregivers' verbal support for the planned intervention.

Reference

McWilliam, R. A. (1991). Targeting teaching at children's use of time: Perspectives on preschoolers engagement. *Teaching Exceptional Children, 23*(4), 42-43.

Bibliography

The following journal articles and books describe in more detail many of the recommended practices in this article.

Betz, C. (1994). Beyond time-out: Tips from a teacher. *Young Children, 49*(3), 10-15.

Carr, E. G., & Durand, V. M. (1985). Reducing problem behaviors through functional communication training. *Journal of Applied Behavior Analysis, 18,* 111-126.

Greenberg, P. (1987). Ideas that work with young children. Good discipline is, in large part, the result of a fantastic curriculum. *Young Children, 42*(3), 49-50.

Greenspan, S. I. (1995). *The challenging child.* New York: Addison-Wesley.

Honig, A. A. (1996). *Behavior guidance for infants and toddlers.* Little Rock, AR: Southern Early Childhood Association.

McCloskey, C. M. (1996). Taking positive steps toward classroom management in preschool: Loosening up without letting it fall apart. *Young Children, 51*(3), 14-16.

Nunnelly, J. C. (1996). *Behavior guidance of three- and four-year-old children.* Little Rock, AR: Southern Early Childhood Association.

Reid, J. (1993). Prevention of conduct disorder before and after school entry: Relating intervention to developmental findings. *Development and Psychopathology, 5,* 243-262.

Rhode, G., Jenson, W. R., & Reavis, H. K. (1992). *The tough kid book: Practical classroom management strategies.* Longmont, CO: Sopris West.

Saifer, S. (1990). *Practical solutions to practically every problem: The early childhood teacher's manual.* St. Paul, MN: Redleaf Press.

Stone, J. G. (1983). *A guide to discipline* (Rev. ed.). Washington, DC: National Association for the Education of Young Children.

Walker, H. M., Colvin, G., & Ramsey, E. (1995). *Antisocial behavior in school: Strategies and best practices.* Pacific Grove, CA: Brooks/Cole.

Addressing Challenging Behaviors at Home

Working With Families to Find Solutions

Gusty-Lee Boulware, M.Ed., Ilene Schwartz, Ph.D.,
and **Bonnie McBride, M.S.,** University of Washington,
Experimental Education Unit

Raising a young child with a disability can be a daunting task. Parents are simultaneously attempting to understand the diagnosis their child has received, deal with their feelings and reactions to the news along with those of their family, sift through the mountains of information they are given (e.g., entering autism or Down Syndrome in any Internet search engine yields thousands of responses), and make decisions about the type of programming their young child will receive. In addition they are continuing to experience the joys and trials of being the parent of a toddler or preschooler. They are dealing with new triumphs and challenges every day—some of which are typical to all young children and some of which are unique to children with disabilities. They are attempting to understand if their child's refusal to sit down to eat dinner is "typical" three-year-old behavior or related to his or her disability, and what they should do in response.

Every day we work with families who inspire us with the love and dedication they demonstrate toward their young children with autism and other severe disabilities. These children provide challenges in many areas: communication, social interaction, play skills, self-care skills, and behavior (Heward, 2000). For many parents, the challenging behavior demonstrated by their young children is one of the most difficult issues they confront. It also is one of the most visible; young children do not get expelled from child care programs because they do not interact with their peers, but they do get expelled when they demonstrate challenging behaviors. The purpose of this article is to explain how we use the principles of positive behavior support to work with families to address challenging behaviors at home and in the community and to share some success stories. We define challenging behavior as behavior that interferes with learning, is dangerous, or is considered problematic by the family.

What Is Positive Behavior Support?

Positive behavior support is an approach to dealing with challenging behaviors that emphasizes prevention, environmental modification, and instruction of appropriate alternative behaviors. According to Koegel, Koegel, and Dunlap (1996), "It was developed in an effort to help people with disabilities and serious problem behaviors with methods that would be effective in changing undesirable patterns of behavior; respectful of a person's dignity; and successful in promoting quality of a person's lifestyle" (p. xiii). In contrast to a more traditional approach to behavior management, positive behavior support assumes that challenging behavior has a communicative function. A goal of positive behavior support is to attempt to understand the function that challenging behavior serves for the child (e.g., attention, escape), and to teach the child a more appropriate behavior that enables him or her to accomplish the same goal (Carr, 1988).

Working With Families to Use Positive Behavior Support

Our use of positive behavior support is based on long-term experience and research with toddlers and preschoolers with severe disabilities in inclusive settings (see the sidebar on page 38 for a description of our current project for young children with autism). One of the topics most frequently identified by families as a high priority is how to address the challenging behaviors their child demonstrates—behaviors that interfere with family life. Our approach to working with families on challenging behaviors has been influenced significantly by the work done in the area of positive behavior support (Fox, Dunlap, & Philbrick, 1997; Horner et al., 1990). Rather than focusing most of the intervention time and attention on eliminating the "problem" behavior, positive behavior support focuses on prevention by identifying the purpose of the challenging behavior, acknowledging and building on the strengths and preferences of the child, reinforcing appropriate behavior, and teaching the child functionally equivalent replacement behavior (Carr, 1988).

This approach often catches parents off guard initially. Parents are ready to tell us about all the different consequences they have tried and are ready for us to tell them what to do. They seem surprised when we start asking about their child's strengths and preferences when the topic is challenging behavior, and even more surprised when we talk about changing the environment and adult behavior as part of the plan to prevent the target behavior. But, once they see the effectiveness of this approach they quickly become its fans. Parents become very skilled at adapting their existing routines to help make their children more successful and are often then able to help other family members and care providers make similar modifications and accommodations to help their children be more successful across environments.

Our approach to working with parents to help them use positive behavior support strategies with their children involves a five-step program (see Table 1). The steps are: (1) identifying the problem, (2) brainstorming, (3) making a plan, (4) implementing the plan, and (5) evaluating the outcomes. We have used this approach with families to address challenging behaviors at home and in the community. We use a combination of parent education meetings and individual home visits to teach parents how to use this process.

Identifying the Problem

The first step of the positive behavior support process is to work collaboratively with the family to identify the problem behavior(s). In some cases, the priority behavior is clear; for example, if a child is aggressive

Table 1

Implementing Positive Behavior Support With Families
1. **Identifying the Problem.** The family and professionals need to agree on what behavior is going to be addressed and be able to identify the behavior reliably across settings.
2. **Brainstorming.** The family and professionals attempt to understand what function the behavior is serving for the child.
3. **Making a Plan.** The purpose of this phase is to figure out how else the child can achieve the function currently being served by the challenging behavior.
4. **Implementing the Plan.** Whatever plan is decided upon by the team must be implemented consistently and correctly across settings.
5. **Evaluating the Outcomes.** Did this plan work? Are all the consumers (e.g., family, professionals) satisfied? What are the next steps?

toward siblings or parents. In many other cases the behavior that is of the greatest concern is difficult for the parents to pinpoint. In the first case study described later in this article, Eric's parents did not have a label for the behavior that resulted in them not wanting to leave their house or do anything that Eric did not like. Although they did not at first consider Eric's behavior across different times of the day related, with the help of a staff member they were able to identify that the common element across all the instances of challenging behavior was an activity change or other type of transition. Once this was identified as the primary concern, the rest of the positive behavior support framework fell into place.

Brainstorming

The next step of the process is to work with the family to understand what the behavior looks like at home, identify a hypothesis about the function of the behavior, and develop ideas about interventions that are acceptable to the family and sustainable at home and in the community. The first part of this process is to ask the family a series of questions about the behavior that we have adapted from the functional assessment interview developed by O'Neill and his colleagues (1997). The questions we ask vary across families and behaviors, but usually include the following, designed to elicit a description of the behavior:
- What does the behavior look and/or sound like? (the topography: frequency; duration; intensity)
- When does the behavior occur?
- When does the behavior *not* occur?
- What happens before and after the behavior?
- How does the child communicate?
- What predicts the behavior?

The answers to these questions guide the rest of the brainstorming process. From this information we can form a preliminary hypothesis about the function (e.g., attention, escape, or sensory input) that the challenging behavior serves for the child.

Making a Plan

In this step we then work with the family to generate possible interventions. We evaluate the ideas from the brainstorming session and decide what to implement. We try to focus the interventions on prevention, or what we can do to help the child be successful in this situation in the future. For example, in the case study about Tyrone (provided later in this article), once we formed the hypothesis that he was taking toiletries to line them up (potentially for sensory input), finding and implementing an appropriate alternative to that behavior was relatively easy for his family.

In forming an intervention plan, we ask parents to consider the acceptability and sustainability of the intervention from the very beginning. We do not want to plan an intervention that is impossible for the parents to implement in a consistent manner. Issues related to the acceptability and sustainability of an intervention comprise the social validity of that intervention (Schwartz & Baer, 1991). The social validity of an intervention is often related to how often or how carefully an intervention is implemented, and the fidelity with which an intervention is implemented is related to its effectiveness (LeLaurin & Wolery, 1992).

An important part of this stage of the process is providing information about positive behavior support and the philosophy on which it is based. We talk about solutions that have worked for this child at school and for other children with similar challenging behaviors. We encourage the family to think about any possible interventions within the context of their ongoing family activities, rituals, and routines. We want them to consider the implications of any proposed intervention on their time, their energy, and their ability to accomplish other demands of family life. Thus, we work with families to select and develop interventions that are reasonable in the context of their lives.

We also work with the parents to figure out every detail of implementing the plan (e.g., what materials will be needed, exactly what to say to the child) and we role play different scenarios depending on the child's possible responses to the intervention. We want parents to be prepared for success, but we also want them to have a plan in case the intervention does not go well the first time they try it.

Implementing the Plan

This part of the process is done by the families and supported by project staff. The amount of support a family receives is determined by the family. In some cases, staff members observe the family implementing the intervention and provide feedback. If parents are interested, we will videotape the intervention and then debrief with the parents while viewing the videotape. In other cases, all of our contact with the family is via the phone. We are in frequent contact with the parents during this stage. We may have daily contact at the beginning of an intervention, and gradually fade out the support as the parents feel more confident in their ability to implement the intervention.

Evaluating the Outcomes

There are two stages to evaluating the outcomes of every positive behavior support plan we develop with families. In the first stage of evaluation we ask questions about the effectiveness of the strategy that was implemented. That is, did it work? Is the child engaging in the challenging behavior less frequently than he or she did before the intervention? Is the child using the functionally equivalent alternative behavior that was taught? Did the intervention result in the child being more independent? Did it reduce the difficulty in caring for the child? For example, if the target behavior was screaming  when the child wanted something and the intervention was to teach the child to exchange picture symbols to make requests, we want to know from the parents if the amount of screaming has gone down (or ideally gone away completely), if the child uses the symbols, and if this new behavior has had an impact on the daily family interactions. If the answer to any of these questions is "no," then we and the family go back to the brainstorming step. For some children with extremely challenging behaviors we may need to go through this process a few times before we devise a strategy that is feasible and effective. If the parents answer "yes" to these initial evaluation questions, we progress to the second stage of the evaluation process.

In the second stage of the evaluation process we work with the family to determine if the problem has been solved to their satisfaction. We remember Baer's (1988) advice that we need to know why we are changing the behavior to determine if we have changed it enough. Since the family members are identifying the problem, they are the only people who can know when we have helped to solve the problem. We use this outcome phase to evaluate what we have accomplished and to help the family set goals for the next step. If the parents are satisfied with the current level of behavior we move on, either to a different challenging behavior or to focus on issues other than challenging behavior. If, however, the parents are not satisfied with the amount of behavior change that has resulted from the current intervention or with other instructional issues related to the intervention, we go back to the brainstorming step and work together to develop a plan for how to further decrease the target behavior or how to decrease the amount of effort necessary to sustain the intervention. During this phase we also remind parents that this is not an easy process. Changing any behavior is hard work, and reducing challenging behavior is difficult for even the most skilled teachers, parents, and therapists.

Positive Behavior Support at Home

Eric's Story: Using Visual Support Strategies at Home

During our first visit with Mr. and Mrs. Bryant, they explained that getting their son Eric, a 32-month old with pervasive developmental disorder, to come into the house after playing in their yard was very challenging, much more so than with their first two children. One of the parents or one of their children would often stay outside with Eric until he entered the house on his own. Typically, when they told Eric it was time to come inside he failed to respond and usually continued to play. The Bryants tried to explain to him in simple language what was coming next (e.g., time for the computer, time to eat). They explained that this never worked with Eric, although it had worked with their two older children when they were that age. At times, they would try to help him

put his toys away, but more often than not Eric would start crying, grab for the toys, and sometimes even hit family members. Often when one of his parents was home alone with him, they would simply carry Eric into the house crying, kicking, and screaming. Both parents expressed how upset it made them to see him cry and how frustrating it  could be for the entire family. They also confided that at times Eric's behavior could be a bit embarrassing when the neighbors were outside watching. However, they both knew that once they could get Eric into the house they could calm him down by presenting an "indoor" activity that he enjoyed (e.g., dinner, computer time, art materials, a video).

As the interview continued, the Bryants explained that Eric demonstrated similar behaviors when it was time to take a bath, get dressed in the morning, or get into the car to leave for an event. Together we determined that each situation required Eric to stop what he was doing and transition to a new event or activity. Next, we brainstormed ideas about why Eric behaved as he did in these particular situations and how we might decrease this behavior. From our discussion, we concluded that since Eric was not able to interpret simple words or phrases at this time, his behavior was most likely not a compliance issue but rather a receptive language issue. He did not understand why he had to stop doing something he liked, as well as not understanding what he would be doing next, so he was communicating via tears, screams, hits, and kicks that he did not want his playing to end.

Together we decided that the Bryants should use photos during transition times in order to let Eric know what was coming next. Mrs. Bryant snapped photos of Eric's favorite Barney™ plate and spoon to signify dinner, his computer and art materials to indicate indoor play activities, the bathtub to indicate a bath, and the car to indicate going somewhere in the car. In this case, our intervention worked beautifully and Mr. and Mrs. Bryant were delighted with the results. Upon presenting a picture to their son, Eric would generally stop what he was doing and often ran ahead of them to the designated area the picture represented. They were both very proud of their son's improved behavior and learned that interpreting visual information was a strength for their son.

Tyrone's Story: Replacing the Challenging Behavior With a More Acceptable Form

At the beginning of each home visit, we routinely ask families, "What's new?" This is a time to share new and exciting things their children have done or, in some cases, challenging situations that have evolved since our last visit. When we asked Cecilia, the mother of a five-year old with autism, this question, she told us that her son's new favorite activity was lining up the family's toiletry items and socks in the living room. This was causing Cecilia much distress and she had tried numerous ways to stop her son, Tyrone, from doing this. She attempted to keep the bathroom door locked, but someone in the family would invariably forget to lock it and Tyrone would get in. She tried locking the bedroom doors, with the same result. She had moved all the toiletry items out of Tyrone's reach, but he figured out a very unsafe way to get to them. She had also tried taking the objects from Tyrone while he was lining them up or after he lined them up. This resulted in a struggle with him grabbing the items from her and crying, while she, in turn, would become upset and sometimes yell.

Cecilia stated that she was at her "wits end" and wondered if we had any advice. Together we brainstormed a strategy to decrease Tyrone's behavior of lining up the toiletries and socks. Since Tyrone did not usually spend too much time with the toiletry items or socks after lining them up, Cecilia was not concerned that he lined up objects. She believed that it helped him to "get his world in order." However, she did mind what objects he was choosing to line up. She also stated that she did not mind the location of where he was lining up the objects. She explained that the living room was the family room and, therefore, liked it when Tyrone spent time in this room. Again, the issue was the objects he was choosing to line up.

We decided that teaching Tyrone to line up age appropriate toys would be more acceptable to Cecilia. Upon inspecting the toys in Tyrone's room, she chose his blocks and cars for use in the intervention. The next steps included anticipating Tyrone's behavior of lining up the socks and toiletries and guiding him to line up the blocks and cars in the exact same spot in the living room. Cecilia provided a lot of social praise as she helped him line up the blocks and cars. Tyrone enjoyed the social praise from his mother. In addition, since he enjoyed her singing, she would often sing as she helped him to line up the blocks and cars. At first Cecilia had to spend the same amount of time with her son teaching him the new routine as she did trying to end the old routine, although this time spent was more pleasurable now that the frustration and yelling had been eliminated. After three days of teaching Tyrone what he could line up by anticipating his behavior, Tyrone was now lining up his blocks and cars in the living room.

During the next visit with the family, Cecilia shared that Tyrone was still lining up the blocks and cars in the living room, but that occasionally he would imitate his older brother's play with the blocks (e.g., making a road with the blocks and driving the cars on it). She believed her intervention efforts were a success. In addition, she learned the valuable strategy of replacing a challenging behavior with a more acceptable one.

Alex's Story: Reinforcing Appropriate Behavior

During one of our parent education meetings, Sarah and Ted shared with the group how frustrating their meal times had become. Since this was an important family routine, they wanted ideas about how to get Alex, their four-year-old son with autism, to come to the dinner table when asked. Currently, his typical behavior included running away from the table during the meal. As a group, we brainstormed ideas about why

Project DATA

Project DATA (Developmentally Appropriate Treatment for Autism) is a federally funded model demonstration project. Our model has five components that work together to yield more positive outcomes for young children with autism and their families:

1. **High Quality Inclusive Early Childhood Program.** The primary component of our program revolves around children's participation in a high quality inclusive early childhood program (Schwartz, Billingsley, & McBride, 1998). This program provides classroom activities that promote successful interactions with typically developing peers, dynamic interactions between children and the environment, and employs a developmental-behavioral approach to instruction and curriculum (Allen & Schwartz, 1996).

2. **Extended Instructional Time.** Children in the program receive approximately 20 hours per week of services at school, 11 hours in the classroom, and nine in an extended day program. This more intensive intervention component, focused on highly individualized instruction, addresses areas of need identified by families and the preschool staff.

3. **Technical and Social Support for Families.** Project DATA has a Family Services Coordinator (FSC) who meets with each family individually to assess needs and priorities.

4. **Collaboration and Coordination Across Services.** The FSC serves as the liaison between the classroom, the extended day program, the family, and any other family-negotiated services (e.g., child care, private speech therapy). This collaboration is important to facilitate optimal outcomes for children and to reduce stress for the families (e.g., Donegan, Ostrosky, & Fowler, 1996; Dunlap, Koegel, & Koegel, 1984).

5. **Transition Support.** The FSC works with the family and the public schools to identify an appropriate program and to ensure that the staff at the receiving school are provided support to prepare for the transition.

this behavior was occurring. Through this discussion, Sarah and Ted determined that Alex did not find sitting at the table as exciting as having his mom or dad chase him.

Once the potential function of the behavior was identified, the focus of the brainstorming session shifted to possible intervention strategies. Another parent in the group had encountered this very same situation and shared her success story. In her case, she knew that her daughter with autism enjoyed dinner by candle light. She taught her daughter that if she came to the table when called, they would light the candles for dinner. This strategy worked, and the entire family enjoyed the ambiance. Sarah and Ted decided this was the strategy they wanted to try. They also decided that if Alex did get out of his seat, they would blow the candles out for the rest of the meal and that Alex would be done with dinner. At our next parent education evening, Sarah and Ted told us that the strategy had worked and that Alex was even sitting at the table when the candles were not lit. Now they only lit the candles every third night or so.

Conclusion

The process we have described for helping parents use positive behavior support at home, and the stories we have shared, have proven to be successful with many children with many types of disabilities including autism. These strategies are not a simple cookbook—they do not tell you what to do for every child who has problems with transitions, for example, but they do offer a framework for working with families to help them solve the challenging behaviors they experience at home and in the community. The positive behavior support strategies are an integral part of our entire program for young children with disabilities, including children with autism. Working with parents to use this process helps parents view their children's behaviors in a different manner. They are able to be more objective about some of the most challenging behaviors; this change in perception often leads to more successful interventions and more positive interactions. The success of this planning process also appears to increase the confidence and competence of parents to tackle challenging behaviors on their own. The end result is that many families feel more confident about taking their children out in the community to discover new, exciting experiences that are usually part of the lives of most families with young children.

Note

Preparation of this manuscript was funded in part by grant #H024B70091, U.S. Department of Education, Office of Special Education Programs (OSEP). Opinions expressed herein are those of the authors and do not necessarily represent the position of the U.S. Department of Education. For more information please contact Ilene Schwartz: ilene@u.washington.edu; University of Washington, Box 357925, Seattle, WA 98195.

References

Allen, K. E., & Schwartz, I. S. (1996). *The exceptional child: Inclusion in early childhood education.* Albany, NY: Delmar.

Baer, D. M. (1988). If you know why you're changing a behavior, you'll know when you've changed it enough. *Behavioral Assessment, 10,* 219-223.

Carr, E. (1988). Functional equivalence as a mechanism of response generalization. In R. Horner, G. Dunlap, & R. Koegel (Eds.), *Generalization and maintenance: Lifestyle changes in applied settings* (pp. 221-241). Baltimore: Paul H. Brookes.

Donegan, M. M., Ostrosky, M. M., & Fowler, S. A. (1996). Children enrolled in multiple programs: Characteristics, supports, and barriers to teacher communication. *Journal of Early Intervention, 20,* 95-106.

Dunlap, G., Koegel, R. L, & Koegel, L. K. (1984). Continuity of treatment: Toilet training in multiple community settings. *Journal of the Association for Persons with Severe Handicaps, 9*(2), 134-141.

Fox, L., Dunlap, G., & Philbrick, L. (1997). Providing individual supports to young children with autism and their families. *Journal of Early Intervention, 21*(1), 1-14.

Heward, W. L. (2000). *Exceptional children: An introduction to special education.* Upper Saddle River, NJ: Merrill.

Horner, R., Dunlap, G., Koegel, R., Carr, E., Sailor, W., Anderson, J., Albin, R., & O'Neill, R. (1990). Toward a technology of "nonaversive" behavior support. *Journal of the Association for Persons with Severe Handicaps, 15*(3), 125-132.

Koegel, L., Koegel, R., & Dunlap, G. (1996). *Positive behavior support.* Baltimore: Paul H. Brookes.

LeLaurin, K., & Wolery, M. (1992). Research standards in early intervention: Defining, describing, and measuring the independent variable. *Journal of Early Intervention, 16,* 275-287.

O'Neill, R., Horner, R., Albin, R., Sprague, J., Storey, K., & Newton, S. (1997). *Functional assessment and program development for problem behavior: A practical handbook.* Pacific Grove, CA: Brooks/Cole.

Schwartz, I. S., & Baer, D. M. (1991). Social-validity assessments: Is current practice state-of-the-art? *Journal of Applied Behavior Analysis, 24,* 189-204.

Schwartz, I. S., Billingsley, F. F., & McBride, B. (1998). Including children with autism in inclusive preschools: Strategies that work. *Young Exceptional Children, 2*(1), 19-26.

First Step to Success

A Collaborative Home-School Intervention for Preventing Antisocial Behavior at the Point of School Entry

Hill M. Walker, Ph.D., University of Oregon
Bruce Stiller, Ph.D., Eugene, Oregon Public Schools
Annemieke Golly, Ph.D., Institute on School Violence Prevention, University of Oregon

Greater and greater numbers of at-risk children are entering the schoolhouse door unprepared for the experience of schooling (Yoshikawa & Knitzer, 1997; Zigler, Taussig, & Black, 1992). The effects on children of societal conditions such as poverty, neglect, abuse, prenatal exposure to drugs and alcohol, and domestic violence are clearly reflected in their behavior characteristics within the context of early schooling. The number of children who have been exposed to one or more of these risk factors has increased substantially in the last two decades (Schorr, 1988).

Early childhood educators are generally not accustomed to seeing children who are extremely aggressive with peers; who are successful at resisting adult influence; who wear gang colors; and who bite, kick, and hit their teachers with clear intent to hurt. As depressing as these behavioral characteristics and trends are, there is hope. We can buffer the effects of exposure to the risk factors (e.g., poverty, neglect, abuse) that encourage these behavior patterns and intervene early to divert at-risk children from an antisocial path. Kazdin (1987) has argued convincingly that there is a developmental window up until about age eight or nine in which to intervene so as to achieve this goal. In order to do so, the intervention must be carefully coordinated and involve the three social agents who have the greatest influence on the developing child: that is, parents and caregivers, teachers, and peers or classmates (Reid, 1993).

The remainder of this article describes the *First Step to Success* early intervention program for at-risk kindergartners who show the soft early signs of an antisocial pattern of behavior. Antisocial behavior involves high levels of aggression, bullying of others, defiance of adults, and, in more mature youths, vandalism, stealing, and self-abuse expressed through involvement with drugs and alcohol. Some of these youths become vulnerable to gang membership and, as they mature, begin using acts of violence to solve problems in their social environment (Patterson, Reid, & Dishion, 1992). It may seem overreaching to attribute the above behavior patterns to kindergarten-level children but there are strong connections between them and their early signs in young children. For example, longitudinal research clearly documents that very young children who show the early signs of this behavior disorder often "grow into it" during the elementary school years and subsequently adopt a delinquent lifestyle in adolescence, becoming dangerous to themselves and others (Patterson, Reid, & Dishion, 1992; Reid, 1993).

The *First Step to Success* program was developed through a four-year federal grant to the senior author from the U.S. Office of Special Education Programs. It was published in 1997 (see Walker et al., 1997). The key components of the *First Step to Success* program are described following. In addition, two factual case studies are presented in which the program was applied to a boy and a girl, both of whom manifested severe behavior problems upon entering school. The key features are:

1. *First Step to Success* requires two to three months for implementation from start to finish and is applied within regular kindergarten and home settings. During this period, only small amounts of teacher and parental time are required daily for implementation.

2. The program is implemented by a professional who can serve kindergarten teachers in a consultative capacity (i.e., early interventionist, early childhood educator, behavior specialist, school psychologist, counselor, social worker, and others). This person will invest approximately 50-60 hours total per case during the program's implementation. Teachers can operate the program as part of their regular teaching and management duties.

3. *First Step to Success* consists of three interrelated modules: (1) proactive, universal screening of all kindergartners to identify those at risk; (2) a school intervention component involving teachers, peers, and parents that teaches the child an adaptive behavior

pattern for school; and (3) a parent training component that assists parents in teaching their child skills that contribute to school success (e.g., cooperation, accepting limits, self-esteem, sharing in school, and so forth).

4. During its development and testing, the *First Step to Success* intervention program was applied successfully to 46 kindergartners and their families. It has also been replicated, to date, in four sites in Oregon, three sites in Washington, and one site in Kentucky.

5. The *First Step to Success* intervention produces very powerful behavior changes in the following areas, as indicated by teacher ratings and direct observations: adaptive behavior, aggressive behavior, maladaptive behavior, and the amount of time spent appropriately engaged in teacher-assigned tasks.

6. Follow-up studies show *First Step to Success* intervention effects persist up to two years beyond the end of the initial intervention period; that is, into first and second grades, where the child has new teachers and peers each year.

7. *First Step to Success* participants (i.e., children, parents, peers, and teachers) report high levels of satisfaction with the program.

Details of the program's three modules are provided following, with concrete examples to help with implementation. The early detection module uses a universal screening procedure so every child in a class has an equal chance to be evaluated and identified for participation. There are four options built into the screening component of *First Step*. The screening options range from simple teacher nomination to use of a three-stage, multiple gating process which combines teacher nominations and rank ordering, teacher ratings, and direct observations in structured and unstructured school settings. At-risk children who emerge through this screening process are nearly always found to be in need of early intervention through a program such as *First Step*.

The school intervention module of *First Step* consists of an adapted version of the program for acting-out children *CLASS: Contingencies for Learning Academic and Social Skills* (Hops & Walker, 1988). The school intervention begins with two 20-minute periods daily and is gradually extended to the whole school day (or half day, as the case may be) over a two- to three-month period. The first phase lasts for five days and is operated by the program consultant. During the two daily 20-minute periods of this phase, the consultant sits close to the target child and monitors his or her behavior closely using a green/red card which serves three purposes: (1) to signal the child as to the appropriateness or inappropriateness of his or her behavior, (2) to record points, and (3) to record praise and bonus points.

If most of the available points are awarded on the green side of the card, the child earns a brief, group activity or privilege (e.g., Simon Says, 7-Up Game) for himself or herself and the rest of the class at the end of the period. If the activity or privilege is earned for both periods, the child can also earn a home privilege prearranged with the parents. By the end of the five-day consultant phase, the child can earn one point for each five-minute block of the daily period(s).

The teacher phase of the program lasts for 15 days and begins on program day six when the classroom teacher assumes control of the program. The teacher operates the green/red card and awards praise and points during regular teaching and classroom management routines. The program consultant serves the teacher in a support role during this phase.

The final phase of the program, maintenance, begins on program day 21 and runs to program day 30. During this phase, the child's improved behavior is maintained for the full day and supported primarily by teacher, consultant, and parental praise.

The home intervention module of *First Step*, called homeBase, begins on program day ten of the school intervention and lasts for six weeks. In this module, the child's parents are enlisted as partners with the teacher and program consultant in helping the child get off to the best possible start in school. The parents are taught how to help their child master six key skills essential to school success: (1) communication and sharing at school, (2) cooperation, (3) limit setting, (4) problem solving, (5) friendship making, and (6) developing confidence.

The *First Step* program consultant is responsible for implementing this component; as a rule, one skill is taught to the parents each week during an hour-long session held in the parents' home. The parents are given a handbook of essential materials and a box of games and activities for use in practicing the skills with their child. The homeBase goals for parents, children, and teachers are as follows: (1) parents—teach the skill, provide daily practice, and reward daily practice; (2) child—learn the skill, practice the skill; and (3) teachers—know the skill, praise use of the skill, and give feedback to parents. The ultimate goal of homeBase is to align educators and parents/caregivers on the same side in helping vulnerable children experience early school success. homeBase has proven to be a very popular component of *First Step* with the professionals and parents/caregivers who have participated in the program.

The case studies of Michael and Anke (see Boxes 1 and 2) are presented to help illustrate some of the program's features. The outcomes of these case studies are representative of how most children respond to the program.

The authors and *First Step* developers have involved hundreds of early interventionists, kindergarten teachers, and parents in the program during the past four years. Feedback from these participants has been uniformly positive. The major obstacle or implementation barrier we've encountered so far centers around parents who don't follow through and/or who are not consistent in their application of the homeBase procedures.

First Step to Success has proven to be an effective and popular intervention with early childhood educators. Since the *First Step* program was developed, the authors have successfully extended its use to children in primary grades one and two without the need for program adaptations. Perhaps the program's greatest strengths are: (1) its ability to provide early detection of children whose problems, if left unattended, will likely severely impair their later school adjustment and quality of life; and (2) its collaborative focus on forging partnerships between parents and teachers in helping children get off to the best possible start in school. The earlier intervention occurs, the more likely it is to be effective and long-lasting. To solve the problems so many children are bringing to the schoolhouse door, it is essential that early detection and intervention resources be concentrated at the point of school entry.

Optional training and technical assistance are available for professionals who wish to implement the program in kindergarten- or primary grade-level classrooms. Information about this option can be obtained by contacting the program's publisher or the senior author. Information about the *First Step* program and its cost can be obtained by contacting the program's publisher.

Box 1

Case Study:
M I C H A E L

Michael was referred to the *First Step to Success* program by his first grade teacher, Mrs. Stephens. Mrs. Stephens stated that Michael frequently refused to participate in classroom activities. He challenged her rules and became defiant when corrected. Sometimes, he would hide his face and look away when given a direction he did not want to follow. He overreacted to minor incidents with other children, becoming angry and lashing out. Thus the other children avoided Michael. Michael did not come to the attention of school support personnel during his kindergarten year, perhaps because his teacher was known for rarely referring children in her class.

The pre-intervention screening showed Michael was academically engaged about 80% of the time. Mrs. Stephens completed ratings on his social behavior (i.e., adaptive behavior, maladaptive behavior, and aggression). Michael received extreme, negative ratings on all three instruments. His scores were as follows: Adaptive=20; Maladaptive=35; Aggression=47. Normal or average scores for children in general on these measures are respectively 35, 14, and 7.

During the classroom intervention, Michael was much more cooperative and positive with his peers. Mrs. Stephens said he enjoyed being the center of attention in class. He came to school with a positive attitude, and was much more responsive to correction. The green/red card was extremely helpful in correcting Michael's challenges to classroom rules. Mrs. Stephens could turn the card to red, ignore Michael's behavior, and avoid a confrontation. Michael would usually comply within 20 seconds when she did this.

Michael's mother, Cindy, was delighted with the results of the program. She noticed that he was beginning to show empathy for others and, as a result, was making friends. On one occasion she stated that, "Michael saw another child fall and went over to see if the other child was okay. He never did that kind of thing before the *First Step* program was used." The homeBase module also helped Cindy feel more confident as a parent. She noticed that many of the ideas for teaching cooperation and setting limits were ideas she was already using, but wasn't sure if she was doing the correct thing. She had read many parenting books, and some of them gave conflicting advice or promoted ideas that were not effective. "These ideas actually work," she stated. Michael especially enjoyed practicing the homeBase skills with his

continued—

mother using the cards and games included in the program. His interactions with her became much more positive during and following the
program.

Following the intervention, Michael's rate of academic engaged
time improved to 95%. His teacher ratings were greatly improved
following exposure to the intervention. Michael is now in second
grade. His teacher and mother report he is continuing the success he
had during the program. He is learning rapidly, making friends, and
continues to respond appropriately when corrected by his teacher.
Michael's postprogram ratings by Mrs. Stephens were: Adaptive=31;
Maladaptive=22; and Aggression=5. Cindy said she would be
delighted to have her younger son participate in the *First Step*
program also.

Box 2

Case Study:
A N K E

Anke was a powerful, controlling kindergarten student who often
refused to follow teacher and parental directions. She dominated her
peers and pouted when she did not get her way. She was referred to
the *First Step* program by her kindergarten teacher, Mrs. Severson.

Anke agreed to play the green/red card game and earned the
chance to sing her favorite song with the class after Session One.
Session Two was held in the computer lab. Anke pounded on her part-
ner's keyboard at the computer. The consultant, sitting right next to
her, turned the card to red. After receiving two points on red, she
continued to hit the keyboard while sticking her tongue out at the
consultant. The consultant kept the card on red without comment.
Anke's behavior escalated. She hid under the desk and pounded the
bottom. The consultant held the red card under the desk. Anke continued to hit, and repeatedly stuck her tongue out at the consultant.
The consultant simply said, "I don't think you are ready to play the
game today," and walked out of the classroom. Anke quickly got out
from under the desk and yelled, "I will play, I will play!" Without
turning around or commenting, the consultant walked out the door.

The teacher reported that, after the consultant left, Anke threw a
fit yelling, "I am ready to play! Why did she have to leave?" The

continued—

teacher ignored Anke and interacted with her again when Anke was calm.

The consultant called Anke's parents that afternoon and informed them that Anke would not be bringing a green/red card home. The consultant instructed the parents that if Anke brought up the incident, the parents were not to discuss the issue but simply say, "I'm sure you will have another chance to play the game tomorrow."

The consultant met with Anke the next day and asked, "Are you ready to play the game today?" Anke said, "I was ready yesterday but you left!" Consultant: "What does it mean when the card is on red?" Anke: "Stop." Consultant: "That's right, you stop and do the right thing. Do you think you can do that?" Anke agreed to play the game. She did a fabulous job.

Anke's behavior improved dramatically during the program. It probably was the first time that an adult did not become involved in a power struggle with Anke. Anke is in fourth grade now. Her current teacher reports it is a joy having her in class and that the other children like her.

References

Hops, H., & Walker, H. M. (1988). *CLASS: Contingencies for learning academic and social skills.* Seattle, WA: Educational Achievement Systems.

Kazdin, A. (1987). *Conduct disorders in childhood and adolescence.* London: Sage.

Patterson, G. R., Reid, J. B., & Dishion, T. J. (1992). *Antisocial boys.* Eugene, OR: Castalia.

Reid, J. (1993). Prevention of conduct disorder before and after school entry: Relating interventions to developmental findings. *Development and Psychopathology, 5*(1/2), 243-262.

Schorr, L. (1988). *Within our reach: Breaking the cycle of disadvantage.* New York: Doubleday.

Walker, H. M., Kavanagh, K., Stiller, B., Golly, A., Severson, H. H., & Feil, E. (1997). *First step to success.* Longmont, CO: Sopris West.

Yoshikawa, H., & Knitzer, J. (1997). *Lessons from the field: Head Start mental health strategies to meet changing needs.* New York: National Center for Children in Poverty.

Zigler, E., Taussig, C., & Black, K. (1992). Early childhood intervention: A promising preventative for juvenile delinquency. *American Psychologist, 47*(8), 997-1006.

Examining the Role of the Classroom Environment in the Prevention of Problem Behaviors

Judy Lawry, M.S.Ed., Cassandra D. Danko, M.S.Ed.,
and **Phillip S. Strain, Ph.D.,** University of Colorado at Denver

As Early Childhood Educators it is likely that we will teach children who exhibit challenging behaviors that test our abilities. Typically, teachers have a "bag of tricks" that they attempt to implement in an effort to address misbehaviors after they have already occurred. These strategies may provide a short term solution but may be ineffective in the long run in preventing the challenging behavior(s) from recurring. Often, teachers are unaware that the more subtle aspects of the classroom's physical and instructional environment are operating to maintain, if not exacerbate, these challenging behaviors.

Through a question and answer format, it is our intention to provide early childhood educators with specific strategies that we have found to be effective in *preventing* challenging behaviors through manipulation of the classroom environment. The following questions were selected based on a combination of the authors' observations during classroom consultations and questions we frequently receive from teachers regarding challenging behaviors. Though many of these strategies may be well known, we have found throughout our work as consultants that it never hurts to be reminded!

Examining the Physical Environment

The physical environment refers to the physical layout of the classroom. The placement of furniture, use of space, or any physical adaptations made to the classroom impact children's level of independence. The size of the classroom, the color of the walls, the type of furniture, the amount of light, and the number of windows may all influence how children will learn (Dodge & Colker, 1996). Consequently, careful arrangement of the physical environment can help to deter challenging behaviors.

"How can I arrange my classroom to prevent frequently occurring problems such as running in the classroom, kids playing with toys when asked not to, children fighting over the same toy, and too many students in one play area?" Questions such as these should serve as indicators that your classroom may be poorly arranged. A classroom with well-defined play areas and clear boundaries is set up to visually remind children where, when, and how to play with materials. Figure 1 provides specific examples of well-defined play areas.

The physical arrangement of the classroom often encourages inappropriate behavior such as running. To help prevent this behavior, limit long and wide open spaces by strategically positioning furniture and by placing visual boundaries on play areas (e.g., using tape on the floor) to clearly delineate where areas begin and end.

Play areas that appear open and inviting may encourage students to grab toys from shelves at inappropriate times of the day. Frequently, children do not realize that it is not time to play with these enticing materials (especially when they are still in the process of learning the daily routine). Teachers can visually close play areas with a blanket or a sheet. Posting a "closed" sign or a "stop" sign at the entrance of a play center can also serve as a visual reminder. Too many students in one play area may result in fighting over toys, an inability to move around the center freely, or limited child-to-child interactions. It is important to restrict the number of children in each play area based on the particular

center's size (e.g., housekeeping may accommodate four children while the computer area may only accommodate two). Limiting the number of children allows them to work successfully in small groups and practice skills like negotiation and problem solving, turn taking and sharing materials, as well

as establishing friendships (Dodge & Colker, 1996). Setting up a system, such as four hooks in each play center that children hang a name card on, provides a concrete cue to children that a center is full.

Figure 1: Bird's-Eye View of Environmentally Inappropriate & Appropriate Classrooms

Classroom A: Environmentally Inappropriate

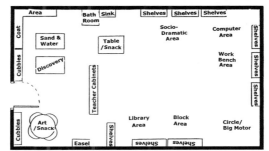

- Art area not near water source
- Toys too close to circle time area
- Quiet centers neighboring noisy areas
- No visual boundaries for play areas
- Unlabeled shelving

- Undefined personal space in circle area
- Snack tables far from each other, limiting social interactions
- Space conducive to running
- Cluttered walls

Classroom B: Environmentally Appropriate

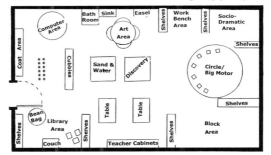

- Visual cues for lining up near door
- Communication pictures pertinent to play area posted for nonverbal children
- Cubbies labeled with photos and names of each child to promote independence
- Shelving labeled to promote independent clean up
- Poster of classroom rules on wall

- Hooks limiting the number of children in each area
- Limited visual stimuli on walls
- Personal visual schedules posted
- Picture of play area at entrance to play area
- Classroom schedule posted
- All shelving/cabinetry low to ground
- (3' high) for staff to see into all areas

"**Structured group time (e.g., circle time) seems to be the most difficult part of the day. How can I set up my circle time area in a way that will prevent challenging behaviors?**" First, ensure that all items (e.g., toy shelves, book shelves) are removed from reach. Turn toy shelves around, cover materials with a blanket, or take materials out of the area entirely. Second, arrange seating patterns to ensure that children are not sitting

too close to one another. Make sure all children are at least one hand apart and can see the activity. Third, use items such as carpet squares, tape squares on the floor, or pictures taped to the floor to visually define each child's physical space.

"**How can I minimize distractions in my classroom?**" Noisy areas are often too close to quiet ones. It is important to physically place quiet areas like the book area, table toys, or writing center away from noisier areas such as housekeeping, gross motor, or block area to help keep noise levels low. In addition, there may be too many visually distracting materials around the classroom, on the walls, and in the play areas. Try to limit such materials and rotate them throughout the school year instead of putting them out all at once. It is purported by Grandin (1995) that some students can be affected by certain types of lighting because they can actually see the flicker in the cycle of electricity. To limit distractions associated with lighting, try avoiding fluorescent lights and opting for indirect lighting or draping material on top of lighting to help create a calming effect. If you must use fluorescent lights, try to use the newest bulbs you can get as they flicker less. Also try placing a child near a window to minimize the effect of the light, but only if the child will not be too distracted by looking outside.

Examining the Instructional Environment

The instructional environment includes the daily routine of the classroom, transition times, the materials available for play at each center, and adult directions given to children. All of these activities are potential times to see problem behaviors. The consistency of the routine, the organization of transitions, the level of motivation to change activities, the kinds of toys available, and the way directions are given will impact the way children respond. Careful planning of the instructional environment can help deter challenging behaviors.

"**What can I do to ensure a smooth flow in the daily routine?**" First, start by examining your daily class schedule. Is it balanced? For example, quiet times vs. active times, small groups vs. large groups, teacher directed vs. child directed. Are activities too difficult without adult assistance? Are activities clearly defined so that students can independently get started? Figure 2 provides an example of a well-balanced daily schedule with descriptions for each activity.

Most children feel safer and more secure when they can count on a consistent daily routine. Children, like most adults, want to know what will happen next. As a result, disruptions in the daily routine can be upsetting and cause tantrum behavior in some children. Children can be

Figure 2: Sample Daily Schedule

8:45-9:00	Table Time	Children have a choice between a theme related project or fine motor manipulatives. The activities are limited to the table area, giving children more structure. This allows children time to organize themselves and make the transition from home to school.
9:00-9:15	Circle Time	Large group activity that focuses on songs, finger plays, and social skills. Activities are sequential and repetitive. Props are used to facilitate socialization between children.
9:15-10:00	Center Time	Children may choose from activities in interest areas as well as participate in teacher-directed individual or small group activities. Play centers include: messy table, discovery, workbench, art, table toys, books, gross motor, housekeeping, blocks and computer.
10:00-10:15	Story Time	A story related to the weekly theme is read to the children. Hands-on props, visual materials, or puppets are used to increase engagement.
10:15-10:30	Snack	Children are assigned roles such as "Drink Captain" and "Snack Captain" to encourage peer to peer interactions.
10:30-10:40	Quiet Time	Children look at books in a cozy, soft, quiet area of the room until everyone has finished snack.
10:40-11:00	Outdoor Play	Children participate in outdoor motor activities.
11:00-11:20	Motor Group	Children choose between three play areas: fine motor (theme related art project), sensory motor (tactile materials) or gross motor (obstacle course).
11:20-11:30	Closing Circle	Children gather as a large group, sing favorite songs, talk about day's events, and prepare to go home.

prepared ahead of time for changes through the use of visual schedules. A pictorial schedule representing the day's events may be attached to a wall in the classroom and, if attached with hook and loop fasteners, easily manipulated as needed. Reviewing the changes at the beginning of the day with the entire class or individually may prevent tantrums from occurring later.

It is common for all of us to have certain times of the day when we function more or less optimally, and children are no exception. Many teachers are committed to keeping the same schedule year after year even though the students are different. Activities should be sequenced by degree of activity level (Whaley & Bennett, 1991). Proper sequencing of activities can positively affect child behavior (Krantz & Risley, 1977). Try altering the schedule to find the best time of the day for each activity. For example, you may want to start the day with a calming activity such as table time instead of an active exercise like outside time. If you notice children having consistent difficulty with the last 30 minutes of the day, you may want to provide them with a choice between a movement activity (obstacle course) in one part of the classroom and a quiet activity (modeling clay) in another part of the room.

"How can I make transition times less noisy and chaotic?" Motivating children to clean up and independently begin the next activity is often quite a challenge. Additionally, if children spend too much time waiting for the next activity to begin they will frequently look for ways to entertain themselves. These problems can be resolved by making the transitions themselves entertaining. Transitions, like other daily activities, should be planned. For example, play an upbeat song and challenge the children to clean up before it ends. Everyone who has cleaned up and is sitting ready for the next activity receives a stamp on their hand. Plan motor activities such as riding scooter boards, wheel barrow walks, or imitating animals to transition to the next activity. Blink the lights or ring a bell as a signal to the children to meet you in the center of the classroom, then sing a song such as, "Touch your head, touch your head, touch your head, clap, clap." This ensures that all of the children have stopped playing and are focused on you as you give the direction to clean up. A teacher can also avoid letting children "entertain themselves" by overlapping activities or having an adult available to greet children, get them started on the next activity, or sing songs with the group until everyone has transitioned.

Some children, particularly children with autism, may have a difficult time understanding or dealing with a transition from one activity or place to another. A child who consistently becomes stressed or cries when it is time to transition may benefit from an individual picture schedule. A picture of the next activity, place, or person paired with verbal instructions may help the child to better process information and prepare for what will happen next.

"How can I motivate children who refuse to clean up or constantly tantrum when it is time to clean up?" The first thing to consider is whether or not children are being given enough time to choose and become deeply involved in activities. Time allotted to play in centers should be longer than any other time of the day (Figure 2). The second thing to consider is whether you give children ample warning that play time will end soon. If you are utilizing these strategies and you still have a child who gets upset when it is time to clean up, you may need to place a buffer activity between a favorite activity and clean-up time. For example, one might coax a child who really loves the sand table to a less desirable activity five minutes before clean-up time. It will be easier for the child to give up the less desirable activity to participate in clean-up.

"How can I increase positive social interactions such as sharing and turn-taking between my students?" Children are often expected to know how to share toys and cooperate with others when they have not been taught specifically how to do so. Teachers should provide duplicates of novel toys and high-demand items *until* social skill training has occurred. A formalized social skills curriculum should be used at the beginning of the school year and reviewed periodically as needed. Skill training may include strategies for getting a friend's attention, sharing, asking for a toy, asking for help, and giving a play idea (Strain, Kohler, Storey, & Danko, 1994). Use puppets and role playing to challenge the children with a social dilemma such as wanting a toy another child has. Encourage children to problem solve ways to ask for the toy. Pair words with strategies such as tapping a friend on the shoulder or holding out a hand to request a toy for children who are nonverbal or language delayed. Adopting a formal way of reinforcing the students or letting them know that you value their use of these skills is an important step in getting them to continue using the strategies. Also, try pairing each child with a peer who exhibits appropriate behaviors and social skills.

"How can I increase 'on-task' behavior and prevent problems such as wandering, boredom, refusal to participate, and poor attending?" There are several reasons why a child may have difficulty getting started with an activity or joining other children in play. The two most common reasons, however, are that the child is bored with the toys/activities or lacks the skills necessary to initiate or sustain play interactions. If the same toys, materials, or activities are used for several weeks in a row, the children will become bored (and when children are bored, they will misbehave). Novelty is the key to preventing boredom. Rotating new toys in and out of the classroom as well as adding theme-related materials to the classroom will capture children's interest and facilitate more active engagement with materials. A toy rotation plan can increase engagement in typical children from 71% to 81% in less than a month (McGee, Daly, Izeman, Mann, & Risley, 1991). New toys can be added inexpensively to the classroom by swapping toys with other teachers, asking parents for donations, or visiting flea markets and thrift stores. Consider setting up a twice a month toy rotation system with two other classrooms in your area.

You will know if your play centers are effective if children are able to: (1) make choices and select activities independently; (2) use available materials appropriately and creatively once inside an area; (3) persist at an activity and remain involved for a designated period of time; (4) feel successful when they play in an area; and (5) help take care of materials (Dodge & Colker, 1996).

Children who refuse to participate in play activities may also be reacting to the structure of the play interactions. Adults tend to think they are "playing" with a child when, in fact, they are merely giving a series of directions. An adult can potentially give a child many directions in a short period of time like, "Johnny, put the man in the boat. Make him follow me. Where is his hat? What color is it? Give me the dog. Share the boat with Suzie." "Play" like this can be boring for children as evidenced by their leaving the area, ignoring your requests, or exhibiting tantrum behavior. Instead, try commenting on or narrating the child's play (e.g., "You put the man in the boat. He is floating down the river. The dog jumped in the boat!).

Wandering from play area to play area may occur when a child lacks the skills needed to engage in play with toys. In some cases, it may be necessary to teach a particular child how to play with toys appropriately prior to teaching him/her ways to interact with other children.

Activities or materials that are not appropriate for children's developmental levels may also result in a refusal to participate or tantrum behavior. When preparing lessons, selecting toys, or choosing activities keep in mind that the age and skill level of each child will be varied. In other words, adaptations will need to be made for some children while other children will be ready for more challenging tasks. For example, if your circle time consists primarily of talking to or reading to the children you will most likely lose the interest of children with language delays or attention deficits. Once you lose a child's interest, he/she may try to leave the activity, lie down, or try to engage another child. Adding visual props and hands-on manipulatives can provide all children, regardless of their skill level, the opportunity to have fun, participate, and learn from the lesson. Furthermore, children who are ready to be challenged can be assigned roles to act out stories with the props, or act as peer teachers by giving directions and helping classmates who need additional assistance.

When preparing large group lessons the following strategies can be used to prevent challenging behaviors and increase student participation: (1) limit structured group times to 15 minutes at the most for preschoolers; (2) add some kinesthetic motor movement to group times and give children chances to respond actively (e.g., clapping, jumping, acting out the story); (3) let children hold an item related to the theme or story or something that provides sensory feedback; (4) supplement your lessons with colorful images and props (i.e., puppets, photos); and (5) vary the intonation and inflection in your own voice to make speech more engaging to the children.

Poor attention and inappropriate behaviors during large group activities may be prevented by utilizing group monitoring strategies. Effective monitoring strategies direct children to maintain appropriate instructional behavior and prevent the teacher from having to interrupt the lesson to attend to a child's behavior. The classroom assistant quietly redirects children back to the lesson by whispering in their ear or by cuing the teacher to attend to a particular child. The classroom assistant is at an advantage in that he/she can watch the entire group and may observe behaviors the teacher may miss while teaching. When monitoring procedures are used effectively the teacher should never have to interrupt a lesson to attend to an inappropriate behavior. Observation of the group should be continual, and if all the children are on task and attending to the teacher, no other intervention may be necessary.

Monitoring strategies are also very effective in helping children who can only sit and attend for brief periods of time. When the teacher is unable to attend to a particular child, the monitor can quietly reinforce that child's behaviors. For example, one might watch the child and every two minutes quietly whisper in his/her ear, "I like the way you are sitting," or "You remembered to raise your hand." The monitor can couple this statement with a touch if physical affection is reinforcing for the child. If a child has been sitting appropriately for a long period of time and has not been called upon or talked to by the teacher, the monitor can cue the teacher, or remind him/her about the child with a small gesture.

Effective group monitoring requires that a second adult be available. Unfortunately, setting up for the next activity is often a priority for the classroom assistant, rather than helping the teacher keep children engaged. This would be a good time to look at the order of your daily routine. Schedule activities that need more preparation time right after play time. Plan ahead by closing a play center or table activity two to three minutes prior to clean-up. This allows the assistant time to set up for the next activity in that area as the children continue to play. The classroom assistant will then be ready and available to monitor children's behavior as they transition to and participate in more structured group activities.

If you do not have a classroom assistant, strategies such as providing visual props (e.g., masks, musical instruments, puppets, small animals) and offering jobs to children (e.g., carpet collector, song selector, line leader) during circle times can be outstanding motivators for children to attend to your lesson. Preparing materials ahead of time will likely be necessary, but the reward will be an attentive, actively participating group of children who all want turns with the novel materials.

"How can I encourage appropriate classroom behavior throughout the day?" Many adults unwittingly fall into the trap of reinforcing inappropriate behavior with their attention. Part of our job as educators is to work on establishing student independence. Hovering over children who tend to misbehave is not a practical solution. As a proactive strategy, try encouraging appropriate behavior by praising the child or offering tangible rewards throughout the day when you see preferred behaviors (e.g.,"Nice sitting quietly, Johnny!"). Build reinforcements into your daily routine such as kids clapping and cheering for one another, gaining access to a favorite item/toy,

or earning a special classroom job. Research has shown that inappropriate behaviors can be dramatically decreased through the use of potent, child-selected reinforcers (Mason, McGee, Farmer-Dougan, & Risley, 1989). Be sure to make a "big deal" about children's appropriate behavior every time you see it initially and plan to gradually decrease the number of times you reinforce.

Finally, teachers can avoid spending too much time "putting out fires" by systematically teaching children the classroom rules at the beginning of the school year. Many teachers address classroom rules as infractions occur. For example, they see a child running and remind the child that running is not permitted. This is a reactive measure rather than a proactive strategy. Classroom rules stated in a positive way should be taught at the beginning of the school year, reviewed and posted as a continual visual reminder. Pictures of the desired behaviors should accompany each written rule (three to four classroom rules should be sufficient for preschoolers). When teaching the rules to children at the beginning of the school year use puppets or encourage the children to act out "breaking the rules." The class can then problem solve what the correct behavior should have been. Another effective strategy is to use rhyming or catchy phrases that children will remember. For example, "When I play inside my school, walking feet are really cool. When I play out in the sun, that's a good time to run and run."

Although this article focuses on changes to the classroom environment, we would be remiss if we did not mention that keeping the lines of communication flowing with the family and other care providers is critical in understanding the *whole child*. Challenging behaviors can be the result of poor eating and sleeping habits or changes in the child's home life. If there is not a chance for regular face-to-face contact or telephone conversations, try implementing a home-to-school journal that addresses issues such as behavior at home, food/diet, sleep, medication(s), changes in the home/family, and other issues you think are pertinent for the particular child. The journal also provides a written record of such information for future reference and identification of patterns of behavior.

Summary

Research has indicated that a carefully managed classroom significantly impacts a child's behavior and functioning (Bailey, Harms, & Clifford, 1983; Dunst, McWilliam, & Holbert, 1986; Twardosz, 1984). The environment can either promote or detract from the efforts of the teacher, classroom assistants, and other team members. The classroom should be arranged not only to support learning but to deter challenging behaviors. It is a good idea to reexamine the physical and instructional environment of your own classroom several times throughout the school year. One way of doing this is by using Figure 3 (on following page) as a tool for self-evaluation.

Figure 3: Classroom Organization and Planning

Key: 5=Super / **3**=Adequate / **1**=Needs Work

1. **Organizes and maintains classroom in an attractive manner**   5   4   3   2   1
   - ☐ maintains a stimulating and orderly environment
   - ☐ ensures that the room and toys are cleaned regularly
   - ☐ sets up and maintains individual interest areas (e.g., sensory table, art, blocks, etc.)
   - ☐ displays children's art work
   - ☐ reduces or removes distracting stimuli when necessary

2. **Maintains an organized daily schedule**   5   4   3   2   1
   - ☐ ensures that daily routine follows an orderly and predictable sequence
   - ☐ considers attention span and abilities of children when planning the length of an activity
   - ☐ posts classroom schedule in an area visible to staff, parents, and outside visitors
   - ☐ follows schedule in a predictable manner but allows for flexibility
   - ☐ provides a balance of activities (active/quiet, teacher directed/child directed, individual/small group/large group)
   - ☐ effectively plans and paces transitions; waiting time is minimal
   - ☐ prepares for transitions; supports children as needed and provides children with sufficient notice that a transition is coming

3. **Arranges the environment and daily routine to support independence** 5   4   3   2   1
   - ☐ sets up and maintains individual interest areas (e.g., sensory table, art, blocks, etc.)
   - ☐ uses low furniture to separate play areas and reduce distraction
   - ☐ labels shelves with pictures of materials to support independent clean-up
   - ☐ places materials on low shelves making them readily accessible to children
   - ☐ establishes a system for children to choose and transition between play areas (name tags, necklaces, clothes pins etc.)
   - ☐ creates a predictable sequence within the daily activities (e.g., circle time includes, "Hello song," introduction of themes, choosing play areas)

4. **Plans easily recognized unit themes**   5   4   3   2   1
   - ☐ selects themes that reflect children's interests and abilities
   - ☐ introduces and discusses themes during large group activities
   - ☐ creatively incorporates and embeds themes into play areas
   - ☐ brings materials related to the theme into the classroom
   - ☐ plans complimentary activities and experiences

continued—

Key: 5=Super / **3**=Adequate / **1**=Needs Work

5. **Encourages teamwork**   5 4 3 2 1

☐ encourages exchange of ideas, sharing observations, and
discussion of new strategies

☐ delineates roles and responsibilities to ensure smooth flow
of daily routine

☐ team meets as a whole to plan for themes and activities
(regular ed & special ed together)

☐ posts staff's duties (weekly) to ensure expectations are
clear plans for all staff members to share in classroom
responsibilities

☐ communicates information regarding child needs, interests
and programming goals with all staff members

Quality Program Guidelines, by D.T. Watson & LEAP Outreach, 1998.
Reprinted with permission.

No single environmental strategy will be sufficient for deterring misbehavior, especially for children with significant challenges, but applying multiple strategies in a consistent manner is a far more efficient and effective approach than responding *after* the fact. We realize that there are many challenging behaviors (e.g., hitting, biting, noncompliance) that are of concern to teachers and that these behaviors are often influenced by factors beyond the scope of the classroom environment. For more information on responding to problem behaviors *after* they have occurred, read *A demonstration of behavioral support for young children with autism* (Dunlap & Fox, 1999).

References

Bailey, D. B., Harms, T., & Clifford, R. M. (1983). Matching changes in preschool environments to desired changes in child behavior. *Journal of the Division for Early Childhood, 7*, 61-68.

Dodge, D. T. & Colker, L. J. (1996). *The creative curriculum* (4th ed.). Washington, DC: Teaching Strategies, Inc.

Dunlap, G., & Fox, L. (1999). A demonstration of behavioral support for young children with autism. *Journal of Applied Behavior Analysis, 1*, 77-87.

Dunst, C. J., McWilliam, R. A., & Holbert, K. (1986). Assessment of the preschool classroom environment. *Diagnostique, 11*, 212-232. New York: Pergamon.

Grandin, T. (1995). *Thinking in pictures*. New York: Random House, Inc.

Krantz, P., & Risley, T. R. (1977). Behavioral ecology in the classroom. In K.D. O'Leary & S.G. O'Leary (Eds.), *Classroom management: The successful use of behavior modification* (2nd ed.) (pp. 349-367). New York: Pergamon.

Mason, S. A., McGee, G. G., Farmer-Dougan, V., & Risley T. R. (1989). A practical strategy for ongoing reinforcer assessment. *Journal of Applied Behavior Analysis, 22*, 171-179.

McGee, G. G., Daly, T., Izeman, S. G., Mann, L. H., & Risley, T. R. (1991). Use of classroom materials to promote preschool engagement. *Teaching Exceptional Children, 23*, 44-47.

Strain, P. S., Kohler, F., Storey, K., & Danko, C. D. (1994). Teaching preschoolers with autism to self-monitor their social interactions: An analysis of results in home and school settings. *Journal of Emotional and Behavioral Disorders, 2*, 78-88.

Twardosz, S. (1984). Environmental organization: The physical, social, and programmatic context of behavior. In M. Hersen, R.M. Eisler, & P.M. Miller (Eds.), *Progress in behavior modification* (Vol. 18, pp. 123-161). New York: Academic Press.

Whaley, K. T., & Bennet, T. C. (1991). Promoting engagement in early childhood special education. *Teaching Exceptional Children, 23*, 51-54.

THE DIVISION FOR EARLY CHILDHOOD

Division for Early Childhood (DEC) Concept Paper on the Identification of and Intervention with Challenging Behavior

Adopted: October 4, 1999
Endorsed by NAEYC: November 1999

Many young children engage in challenging behavior in the course of early development. The majority of these children respond to developmentally appropriate management techniques.

Many young children, including children with disabilities, engage in behavior that is labeled by adults as "challenging." Sometimes, this behavior is short-term and decreases with age and use of appropriate guidance strategies. Additionally, what is "challenging" to one person may not be to another. It is critical for professionals to be aware of and sensitive to how families, cultural groups, and communities define appropriate and inappropriate behavior in young children. Different communities have varying expectations for child behavior. Professionals must respect family, cultural, and community expectations in identifying problems and designing interventions. However, sometimes families or professionals may have inappropriate expectations for young children's behavior. It is important to understand what behaviors are typically associated with particular age groups. For instance, adults need to understand that young children engage in behaviors that older children do not, such as throwing toys or sitting for only short periods of time. With guidance and instruction most children will learn appropriate alternative behavior. Adults must also explore their own beliefs and emotions about certain behaviors (e.g., cursing or hurting others) in order to respond objectively to children. In summary, care must be taken to consider cultural and community beliefs, developmentally appropriate expectations and one's own beliefs about behavior, in the identification of children's behavior as "challenging."

Regrettably, some children's challenging behaviors are not effectively addressed by adult vigilance and use of appropriate guidance strategies. For these children, the challenging behavior may result in injury to themselves or others, cause damage to the physical environment, interfere with the acquisition of new skills, and/or socially isolate the child (Doss & Reichle, 1989; Kaiser & Rasminsky, 1999). It is clear that challenging behaviors such as these seldom resolve themselves without systematic intervention (Kazdin, 1987; Olweus, 1979; Wahler & Dumas, 1986). Relatedly, there is growing evidence that many young children who engage in chronic, highly challenging behaviors proceed through a predictable course of ever-escalating challenging behaviors (Patterson & Bank, 1989; Reid, 1993). What intervention efforts are available for a child who engages in serious challenging behavior?

DEC believes strongly that many types of services and intervention strategies are available to address challenging behavior.

Children may well engage in challenging behavior that quite often can be eliminated by a change in adult behavior. It is possible that the child is reacting to adult behaviors such as lack of attention or unrealistic expectations. By changing adult behavior, we may *prevent* a child's need to engage in challenging behavior. Prevention is the best form of intervention (Poulsen, 1993; Zirpoli & Melloy, 1993). It is time and cost-efficient, and appears to be a major avenue by which to eliminate, not merely reduce, the incidence of challenging behaviors (Strain, Steele, Ellis, & Timm, 1982). Prevention means that the important adults in the child's life have to look at their behavior in the classroom, home, or community setting that might be maintaining the child's challenging behaviors (McEvoy, Fox & Rosenberg, 1991; Strain & Hemmeter, 1997). For example, are toddlers expected to sit through a 30-minute circle time? Is a child getting a cookie when he screams? Effective prevention strategies that have been applied to the challenging behaviors of young children have included systematic efforts to teach parents to use child behavior management skills (Timm, 1993) and efforts to teach alternative, appropriate behaviors that are coordinated between programs *and* home (Walker, Stiller, & Golly, 1998).

Given the nature of most challenging behavior, we believe that there is a vast array of supplemental services that can be added to the home and early education environment to increase the likelihood that children will learn appropriate behavior. A variety of intervention strategies can be implemented with either formal or informal support. Services and strategies could include, but are not limited to: (a) designing environments and activities to prevent challenging behavior and to help all children develop appropriate behavior; (b) utilizing effective behavioral interventions that are positive and address both the form and function of a young child's challenging behavior; (c) adopting curricular modification and accommodation strategies designed to help young children learn behaviors appropriate to their settings; and (d) providing external consultation and technical assistance or additional staff support, e.g. with appropriately trained early childhood special educators. In addition, all professionals who work with children in implementing individualized education programs (IEPs) or individualized family service plans (IFSPs) must have opportunities to acquire knowledge and skills necessary for effective implementation of prevention and intervention programs.

Family members and professionals should work together to identify the challenging behavior, assess it in the settings where it occurs, and design interventions that are realistic to implement and empirically sound. There are literally dozens of empirically validated interventions designed to decrease the challenging behaviors of young children. Effective interventions include the following features:

Comprehensive—It is seldom the case that one intervention strategy will be sufficiently powerful to yield a satisfactory change in challenging behaviors. Therefore, *a comprehensive approach* is highly recommended. For example, a preschool teacher may find that a comprehensive intervention package comprised of the following strategies for teaching children to share will yield far more favorable outcomes than any one strategy used in isolation: (a) Adaptations to activities—a part of opening circle and storytime is devoted to teaching sharing skills; (b) Rehearsal of class rules—sharing is added to class rules and children are reminded of all rules prior to each class transition; (c) Role-playing alternative behaviors—from a prevention perspective, all children are given opportunities to practice sharing and other class rules at the end of opening circle and at the beginning of storytime. From an intervention perspective, squabbles over toys and materials are responded to by having the parties practice appropriate sharing; (d) Arranging for peer models/reinforcing desirable behaviors—many times throughout the day, all children could be found following all class rules, including sharing. When sharing is observed, the teacher communicates in a very positive and public fashion about who is sharing and how they are sharing.

Individualized—Like all other areas of intervention programming, *individualization* is key to success with challenging behaviors. While there is great appeal to the simple formula approach to challenging behaviors (e.g., if Sally does this behavior, you do this), it is a formula doomed to failure. There is overwhelming evidence that children do the same challenging behaviors (e.g., screaming) for fundamentally different reasons and that they may also engage in completely different challenging behaviors (e.g., running away; hitting peers) for the same reason (Carr & Durand, 1985). Therefore, it is imperative to know, at the individual child and specific behavior level, the probable motivations or functions for the challenging acts. For example, a child may scream and cry because she wants more attention, or because she does not want to do something asked of her. The "form" of the behavior is crying. But there are two "functions" described above (attention and escape) that would require different interventions. When choosing an intervention it is critical to assess both what (form) the behavior is and why (function) the child is exhibiting the behavior [see O'Neill, Horner, Albin, Storey, & Sprague (1990) for in-depth descriptions of methods used to identify the specific communicative intent or function of challenging behaviors]. Once this assessment process is complete, an individualized set of strategies can be developed and implemented.

Positive Programming—Because many challenging behaviors elicit such strong emotional responses and at times poor behavior choices by caregivers and teachers, it is essential to focus on the positive aspects of programming (Neilson, Olive, Donovan & McEvoy, 1998). Positive programming refers to: (a) teaching appropriate social skills (e.g., entering play groups); (b) teaching children to self-evaluate and self-monitor their behavior (e.g., am I saying nice things?); and (c) teaching specific communicative *alternatives* to challenging behaviors (teaching a child who tantrums at clean-up time to sign or say "more"). This positive teaching focus also reflects the now accepted and empirically validated notion that many challenging behaviors stem directly from lack of skill in the social and communicative domains.

Multi-Disciplinary—It is also the case that the challenging behaviors of some children clearly demand the input and expertise of *multiple disciplines*. Early childhood special educators, early childhood educators and psychologists are typical members of a team. Pediatricians, neurologists, and child psychiatrists, for example, can also play useful roles in those complex instances where the child's challenging behaviors have a known or suspected neurobiological basis (Hirshberg, 1997/1998). The speech therapist is an essential member of the intervention team when the behavior may be a result of frustration with speech/language difficulties. The role of a team approach is crucial. Just as it is unlikely that a singular educational intervention will be sufficient to manage serious challenging behaviors, it is also unlikely that a biomedical or pharmacological or some other intervention alone will be sufficient.

Data-based—A reliable, viable, and useful system of *data collection* is essential to the success of any intervention plan (Kaiser & Rasminsky,

1999). Data collection can serve many purposes specifically related to challenging behavior. As we indicated above, challenging behaviors often elicit strong, emotional responses from the adults in a child's life. These responses make it difficult for us to be objective about the severity or frequency of a challenging behavior and also can prevent us from recognizing a child's progress related to the challenging behavior. For example, a teacher or parent may be struggling to reduce the spitting behavior of a young boy. The child spits when apparently happy, upset, angry, when hugged, when scolded. When the behavioral consultant asks how often the child spits, the answer is "all the time." In fact, the child is observed to spit 70 to 100 times per day, or put differently, he spits for less than 2 minutes in the four-hour data collection period. To adults this level of spitting indeed feels like "all the time." However, the data collection details the actual frequency as well as other important facts. Data collection can assist us in identifying the frequency of the challenging behavior, contextual variables that may be supporting the child's challenging behavior, and changes that may be needed in the environment to reduce the occurrences of the challenging behavior. In addition, data collection can be used to determine the extent to which an intervention or change in the environment is having a positive effect on the child's behavior. Finally, a data collection system, if designed correctly, increases the likelihood that the adults across the child's environments are addressing the challenging behavior in a consistent way. DEC believes strongly that families play a critical role in designing and carrying out effective interventions for challenging behavior.

Given the family-focused nature of early childhood education, we acknowledge the central role that families play in addressing challenging behavior. Often times, challenging behavior occurs across places, people, and time; thus, families are critical members of the intervention team. A coordinated effort between family members and professionals is needed to assure that interventions are effective and efficient and address both child and family needs and strengths. All decisions regarding the identification of a challenging behavior, possible interventions, placement, and ongoing evaluation must be made in accordance with the family through the IEP, IFSP, or other team decision-making processes.

Often, families *are blamed* for a child's problem behavior. In an extensive review of the literature concerning families of preschool children with conduct problems, Webster-Stratton (1997) confirmed that certain parental/family factors including depression, substance abuse, aggression, antisocial behavior, intense marital conflict, insularity, and ineffective parenting skills appear related to the presence of behavior problems for some children. However, a growing body of evidence was cited in which other factors such as child physiological/ neurological/neuropsychological attributes, communication competence, child social problem-solving skill deficiencies, family poverty, and school setting characteristics also appear directly related to the presence or absence of challenging behavior in children. The most promising emerging perspective within this literature emphasizes the complex interplay among risk factors leading to the formation and perpetuation of problem behaviors.

While the family may or may not have contributed directly to the creation of the challenging behavior, family members are almost always *significantly affected* by the behavior. Webster-Stratton (1990) found that families of children with serious behavioral problems reported the presence of major stressors in their lives two to four times more frequently than did families with typically developing children. Family members are likely to receive unsolicited advice with every tantrum, outburst and misbehavior. Activities that other families seem to enjoy as a matter of course are unattainable or are in constant jeopardy. Isolation becomes a fact of life.

As described earlier, families of children with challenging behavior require access to a *range of* intervention services that are *coordinated* to meet their specific needs. Nicholas Hobbs (1982) observed that "The way one defines a problem will determine in substantial measure the strategies that can be used to solve it" (p. 182). Obviously, if a preponderance of researchers, policy-makers, and practitioners are convinced that families deserve blame for the existence of most challenging behavior, then available services will be structured accordingly. But even if the question of blame is eliminated, there is reason to be concerned that other differences in professional beliefs regarding challenging behavior can create comparable difficulties for families. Advocates of psychopharmacological versus behavioral interventions, homeopathic versus traditional medical treatments, family-centered versus child-centered approaches, or center-based versus home-based service delivery systems collectively produce a bewildering array of disjointed information and difficult choices. Many families of children with challenging behavior have astounding stories to tell regarding their journeys through this landscape of conflicting diagnoses, bickering professionals, and expensive mistakes. There are some children whose problematic behavior is controlled most immediately by physiological factors. There are some individuals who might benefit from appropriate psychopharmacological treatment in order to respond to complementary environmental, curricular, or behavioral interventions. Therefore, as noted earlier, professionals must be aware of the various disciplines and services that might serve as appropriate resources to the family (Reichle, McEvoy, Davis, Feeley, Johnston & Wolff, 1996). All professionals have a fundamental obligation to provide accurate information and support to families as multiple approaches and options are considered.

Finally, families need *partners*. Dunst, Trivette, and Deal (1988) proposed that within the working relationship involving families and early intervention professionals "It is not simply a matter of whether family needs are met, but rather the manner in which needs are met that is likely to be both enabling and empowering" (p. 4). Parents of children with challenging behavior are often frustrated with the child, other family members, and themselves. The understanding and support of professionals can have a profound and positive impact. They need effective tools to use, appropriate resources for support, and assurance that they and their child are accepted.

Professionals and families must carefully evaluate a child's behavior. The focus must be on promoting positive behavior and preventing challenging behaviors. In the appropriate identification of challenging behaviors, consideration must be taken of cultural and community beliefs, developmentally appropriate expectations, and an examination of one's own belief about behavior. When intervention is needed, such interventions must be developmentally, individually, and culturally appropriate. They should be comprehensive, individualized, positive, multi-disciplinary, and consider families as integral to all decisions related to the planning and implementation of the strategies and services.

Note
This concept paper is the result of a work group of DEC members: Linda Brault, Judy Carta, Mary Louise Hemmeter, Mary McEvoy, Shelley Neilsen, Beth Rous, Barbara Smith, Phil Strain, and Matt Timm.

References
Carr, E. G., & Durand, V. M. (1985). Reducing problem behaviors through functional communication training. *Journal of Applied Behavior Analysis, 18*, 111-126.

Doss, L. S., & Reichle, J. (1989). Establishing communicative alternatives to the emissions of socially motivated excess behavior: A review. *Journal of the Association for Persons with Severe Handicaps, 14*, 101-112.

Dunst, C., Trivette, C., & Deal, A. (1988). *Enabling and empowering parents.* Cambridge, MA: Brookline Books.

Hirshberg, L. M. (1997/1998). Infant mental health consultation to early intervention programs. *Zero to Three, 18*(3) 19-23.

Hobbs, N. (1982). *The troubled and troubling child.* San Francisco: Jossey-Bass.

Kazdin, A. (1987). *Conduct disorders in childhood.* Newbury Park, CA: Sage.

Kaiser, B., & Rasminsky, J. S. (1999). *Meeting the challenge: Effective strategies for challenging behaviors in early childhood environments.* Washington, DC: NAEYC

McEvoy, M. A., Fox, J. J., & Rosenberg, M. S. (1991). Organizing preschool environments: Effects on the behavior of preschool children with handicaps. *Education and Treatment of Children, 14*, 18-28.

Neilson, S., Olive, M., Donovan, A., & McEvoy, M. (1998). Challenging behavior in your classroom? Don't react, teach instead! *Young Exceptional Children, 2*(1), 2-10.

Olweus, D. (1979). Stability of aggressive reaction patterns in males: A review. *Psychological Bulletin, 86,* 852-875.

O'Neill, R. E., Horner, R. H., Albin, R.W., Storey, K., & Sprague, J. R. (1990). *Functional analysis: A practical assessment guide.* Pacific Grove, CA: Brooks/Cole.

Patterson, G. R., & Bank, L. (1989). Some amplifying mechanisms for pathological processes in families. In M. R. Gunnar & E. Thelen (Eds.), *Systems and development: The Minnesota symposia on child psychology,* (Vol. 22, pp. 167-209). Hillsdale, NJ: Erlbaum.

Poulsen, M. K. (1993). Strategies for building resilience in infants and young children at risk. *Infants and Young Children,* 6(2) 29-40.

Reichle, J., McEvoy, M., Davis, C., Feeley, K., Johnston, S., & Wolff, K. (1996). Coordinating preservice and inservice training of early interventionists to serve preschoolers who engage in challenging behavior. In R. Koegel, L. Koegel, & G. Dunlap. (Eds), *Positive behavioral support* (pp. 227-264). Baltimore, MD: Paul H. Brookes.

Reid, J. (1993). Prevention of conduct disorder before and after school entry: Relating interventions to developmental findings. *Development and Psychopathology, 5,* 243-262.

Strain, P. S., & Hemmeter, M. L. (1997). Keys to being successful when confronted with challenging behaviors. *Young Exceptional Children,* 1(1), 2-9.

Strain, P. S., Steele, P., Ellis, T., & Timm, M. A. (1982). Long-term effects of oppositional child treatment with mothers as therapists and therapists trainers. *Journal of Applied Behavior Analysis, 15,* 163-169.

Timm, M. A. (1993). The regional intervention program. *Behavioral Disorders, 19,* 34-43.

Wahler, R., & Dumas, J. E. (1986). "A chip off the old block:" Some interpersonal characteristics of coercive children across generations. In P. Strain, M. Guralnick, & H. M. Walker (Eds.), *Children's social behavior: Development, assessment and modification* (pp. 49-91). Orlando, FL: Academic Press.

Walker, H. M., Stiller, B., & Golly, A. (1998). First step to success. *Young Exceptional Children, 1,* 2-7.

Webster-Stratton (1997). Early intervention for families of preschool children with conduct problems. In M. Guralnick (Ed.), *The effectivenesss of early interventions* (pp. 429-453). Baltimore, MD: Paul H. Brookes.

Webster-Stratton (1990). Stress: A potential disruptor of parent preceptions and family interactions. *Journal of Clinical Child Psychology, 19,* 302-312.

Zirpoli, T. J., & Melloy, K. J. (1993). *Behavior management: Applications for teachers and parents.* New York: Merrill.

Permission to copy not needed—distribution encouraged.

Resources
for Children With
Challenging Behavior

Here you'll find additional resources for working with young children with challenging behaviors. Resources range in price. Many are within an individual's budget and others may be more suitable for an agency or school's acquisition.

Gail E. Joseph, M.Ed., University of Washington, and **Camille Catlett, M.A.,** University of North Carolina at Chapel Hill

Books

The Explosive Child: A New Approach for Understanding and Parenting Easily Frustrated, "Chronically Inflexible" Children
by R.W. Greene

Drawing upon recent advances in the neurosciences, Dr. Greene, a child psychologist at Massachusettes General Hospital and Harvard Medical School, describes the factors that contribute to "inflexible-explosive" behavior in children and why the strategies that work for most children aren't as effective for inflexible-explosive children. With the help of vignettes from the lives of children, parents, and teachers with whom he has worked over the years, Dr. Greene lays out sensitive, practical, effective, systematic approaches to helping these children at home and school. This book may help you regain your sanity and optimism as well as rebuild your confidence to handle your child's difficulties. Hardcover. New York: Harper Collins.

Functional Assessment and Program Development for Problem Behavior: A Practical Handbook
by R.E. O'Neill, R.H. Horner, R.W. Albin, K. Storey, & J.R. Sprague

This guide to functional assessment procedures includes a variety of strategies for assessing problem behavior situations, and presents a systematic approach for designing behavioral support programs based on those assessments. Professionals and students together will appreciate the style the authors use to help readers learn to conduct functional assessments and develop their own intervention programs. Pacific Grove, CA: Wadsworth Publishing.

The Incredible Years: A Trouble-Shooting Guide for Parents of Children Aged 3-8
by C. Webster-Stratton

The Incredible Years is a practical guide, filled with examples of everyday problem situations and concerns, and step-by-step suggestions on how to handle them. It is based on over 12 years of detailed research with more than 1000 families as well as Dr. Webster-Stratton's personal experience as a child psychologist, teacher, and parent. Readers will find advice on: How to manage your own anger and frustrations; How to cope with specific problem behaviors such as disobedience, lying, TV addiction, bedwetting, stealing, and others; How to play with your child; How to use praise and rewards to promote good behavior; and How to communicate effectively with your child. Also available on tape in English, Spanish, and Vietnamese. Toronto, Ontario, Canada: Umbrella Press.

More of Dr. Webster-Stratton's resources (including her parenting curriculum and children's Dinosaur School) are available on her Web site: http://www.incredibleyears.com.htm

Meeting the Challenge: Effective Strategies for Challenging Behaviors in Early Childhood Environments
by B. Kaiser & J.S. Rasminsky

Even experienced practitioners need the proven strategies in this book to succeed with those children whose behaviors present particularly tough challenges. It offers easily understandable ideas and approaches that have proven effective for children with challenging behaviors in a variety of settings. Ottawa, Ontario, Canada: Canadian Child Care Federation. Available from NAEYC.

Practical Guide to Solving Preschool Behavior Problems, 4th Ed.
by E.L. Essa

This book presents unique and easy-to-follow information for working with young children with behavior problems and includes a new focus on working with children with disabilities and special needs. The book presents more than 40 behavior problems with examples and explanations, allowing the reader to pinpoint an approach for each specific problem. This fourth edition includes step-by-step instructions on how to help children change misbehaviors. A *Practical Guide to Solving Preschool Behavior Problems* is ideal for professionals who work with a variety of children. New York: Delmar.

Supporting Children With Challenging Behaviors: Relationships Are Key

Supporting Children is a training guide that provides Head Start teaching staff, home visitors, family service workers, managers, and other Head Start staff, as well as consultants, with a process for reflecting on their own practice, assessing difficult situations, and designing interventions through collaborative problem solving. The effective strategies presented in the context of classroom examples build upon what teachers already know and developmentally appropriate practice. (Free for individuals working in Head Start). Washington, DC: U.S. Government Printing Office.

Troubled Families—Problem Children: Working With Parents: A Collaborative Process
by C. Webster-Stratton & M. Herbert

This book helps professionals understand the most effective "therapeutic processes" for supporting families who have children with conduct problems. What sets this book apart is its careful attention to, and elucidation of, the "collaborative process" in working with these children with oppositional and defiant behaviors and their families. In essence, this book illustrates how to empower the parents and to teach them to cope more effectively with their child. This book is used mainly as a text so it is a bit costly, however, it remains a must have for any professional working with children with challenging behavior. Chichester, England: John Wiley and Sons.

Other Resources

First Step to Success: Helping Young Children Overcome Antisocial Behavior
by A. Golly, B. Stiller, E.F. Feil, H.H. Severson, H.M. Walker, & K. Kavanaugh

This program was developed specifically for kindergartners who either display an antisocial behavior pattern or show clear signs of developing one. *First Step* is an early intervention program based on best-practices designed to divert at-risk children from a path leading to an antisocial pattern of behavior. *First Step* is a joint home and school intervention that enhances early school experiences and assists at-risk children in getting off to the best start possible by enlisting the coordinated support and participation of the three social agents who are most important in their lives: parents, teachers, and peers. Based on years of research with hundreds of young children this intervention program is highly recommended for any early childhood classroom.

> Sopris West
> 4093 Specialty Place
> Longmont, CO 80504
> (800) 547-6747
> FAX: (303) 776-5934
> http://www.sopriswest.com

Project Relationship: Creating & Sustaining a Nurturing Community
by M.K. Poulsen & C.K. Cole

This 41-minute (5 segment) video tape depicts a family and professionals working together to meet the needs of a young child with significant behavioral issues. Along with accompanying written material, it provides a nice model for practitioners who want to develop their skills for planning effectively with families.

> Los Angeles Unified School District
> Infant and Preschool Programs
> Division of Special Education
> 936 Yale Street
> Los Angeles, CA 90012
> (213) 229-4713

Reframing Discipline: Educational Productions

Reframing discipline is a series of three video-based training programs for any early childhood professional. Each program is divided into a teaching tape that presents footage of real teachers practicing the strategies, and a practice tape and manual that allow viewers to apply what they've learned in the teaching tape. The content is varied in skill level so novice to veteran early childhood professionals will gain new insights into working with children with challenging behavior. Unfortunately, videos of this caliber are not inexpensive to produce so they are a bit costly—but a great investment for a center or school. Portland: Educational Productions.

http://edpro.com.htm

Samantha
by G. Devault, C. Krug, A. Turnbull, & R. Horner

This video offers very useful instructional examples of creating a successful positive behavioral support plan for a nine-year-old girl with autism. The accompanying print material (*Why Does Samantha Act Like That? A Positive Behavior Support Story of One Family's Success*) tells the family story and includes plan charts and other instructional material. Lawrence, KS: Beach Center on Families and Disability.

The Beach Center on Families and Disability
The University of Kansas
3111 Haworth • Lawrence, KS 66045
(785) 864-7600 • FAX (785) 864-7605
http://www.lsi.ukans.edu/beach/beachhp.htm

Web Site Resources

Family Connection Research Brief: Challenging Behavior and Inclusion (Beach Center)

Available online at http://www.lsi.ukans.edu/beach/html/s9.htm

National Association of School Psychologists

The NASP website has information on topics related to positive behavioral support.

Available online at http://www.naspweb.org/center.html

Positive Behavioral Support

(1997). *Beach Center Newsletter, 8*(3). Lawrence, KS: Beach Center on Families and Disability. This issue is entirely devoted to positive behavioral support.

> Available online at http://www.lsi.ukans.edu/beach/html/pbs.htm

U.S. Office of Special Education Programs (OSEP)
Center for Positive Interventions and Behavior Supports

The OSEP Center on Positive Behavioral Interventions and Supports is a web site containing information on Functional Behavioral Assessments, school-wide PBS, Classroom Support, Individual Support, Conferences, and Related Links. PBS is not a new intervention package nor a new theory of behavior, but an application of a behaviorally-based systems approach to enhancing the capacity of schools, families, and communities to design effective environments in which teaching and learning occurs.

> Web site: http://www.pbis.org

Division of Early Childhood (DEC) – Who We Are

The Division for Early Childhood (DEC) of the Council for Exceptional Children (CEC) is a national, nonprofit membership organization of individuals who work with or on behalf of children with special needs, birth through age eight, and their families. Founded in 1973, DEC is dedicated to promoting policies and practices that support families and enhance the optimal development of children. Children with special needs include those who have disabilities, developmental delays, are gifted/talented, or are at risk of future developmental problems.

DEC offers a variety of products and services related to early childhood education/intervention.

- *Journal of Early Intervention:* Quarterly journal with current research and issues, book reviews, legislative events, and technological information
- *Young Exceptional Children:* Quarterly publication with practical ideas for teachers, therapists, parents, and administrators
- *Young Exceptional Children* Monograph Series No. 1: Practical Ideas for Addressing Challenging Behaviors
- *Young Exceptional Children* Monograph Series No. 2: Natural Environments and Inclusion
- *Recommended Practices in Early Intervention/Early Childhood Special Education:* Coming in December 2000
- Position Papers
- Regional Training Series
- Annual Conference

Division for Early Childhood
27 Fort Missoula Road, Suite 2 • Missoula, MT 59804
(406) 543-0872 phone • (406) 543-0887 fax
Email dec@dec-sped.org • Website www.dec-sped.org

y**O**u**n**g
E x c e p t i o n a l
children

The Young Exceptional Children (YEC) Monograph Series is designed for teachers, early care and education personnel, administrators, therapists, family members, and others who work with or on behalf of children, ages birth to eight, who have identified disabilities, developmental delays, are gifted/talented, or are at risk of future developmental delays or school difficulties.

One of the goals of the Series is to translate evidence-based findings into effective and useful strategies for practitioners and families. Articles in the YEC Monograph Series have a sound base in theory or research, yet are reader-friendly and written for a broad audience.

Monograph Series No. 1 –
Practical Ideas for Addressing Challenging Behaviors
These articles offer proven interventions for challenging behaviors that can be used in early childhood programs and at home. Articles cover such topics as identification, prevention, environmental modifications, instruction of appropriate alternative behaviors, and more. *G143MONO1*

Monograph Series No. 2 – Natural Environments and Inclusion
With IDEA '97 prompting inclusive settings for children with disabilities, it is important to consider the natural settings in which these children are being taught and cared for—child care centers and preschools in particular. These articles include strategies for implementing effective individualized intervention within inclusive settings, ways to ensure that early childhood programs nurture positive attitudes and provide valuable experiences, and examples of state and federal regulations that clarify changes in early intervention. *G143MONO2*

Monograph Series No. 3 – Teaching Strategies
The focus of this issue is on effective and doable teaching strategies that teachers can use in their early childhood classrooms or centers. Articles highlight teaching practices for a variety of curriculum content. *G143MONO3*

Monograph Series No. 4 –
Assessment: Gathering Meaningful Information
Translating research findings into effective and useful assessment strategies is often a difficult and tedious task for practitioners and families. These articles provide practical ideas for conducting meaningful assessments of young children such as linking assessment to intervention planning; involving families in the assessment process; evaluating the impact of culture and language on assessment; and social, behavioral, and functional skills. *G143MONO4*

Monograph Series No. 5 – Family-Based Practices
The articles in this issue demonstrate effective strategies that increase the sharing of responsibility and open communication between parents and professionals. Complementing DEC Recommended Practices, this book offers methods, supports, and resources that strengthen family functioning. *G143MONO5*

Monograph Series No. 6 – Interdisciplinary Teams
The articles in this monograph highlight practices found in Chapter 4 (Trivette & Dunst, 2000) of *DEC Recommended Practices in Early Intervention/Early Childhood Special Education* (Sandall, McLean, & Smith, 2001). They address the values, beliefs, and practices inherent in the *Recommended Practices* definition by describing specific strategies that will assist practitioners to collaborate with families in achieving the various components of the *Recommended Practices*. *G143MONO6*

Monograph Series No. 7 –
Supporting Early Literacy Development in Young Children
The seventh issue in the series addresses the support of early literacy development in young children. The articles in this monograph provide guidance to early educators, family members, and caregivers as they seek to support the development of literacy in the young children in their care. *G143MONO7*

SOPRIS
WEST™
EDUCATIONAL SERVICES

A Cambium Learning™ Company

Phone: (800) 547-6747
Fax: (888) 819-7767
www.sopriswest.com

DEC Recommended Practices

A Comprehensive Guide for Practical Application

in Early Intervention/
Early Childhood
Special Education

Bridging the gap between research and practice, the book *DEC Recommended Practices* provides guidance on effective practices for working with young children with disabilities. The recommended practices are based on a review and synthesis of the research literature and the practices identified as critical by various stakeholders in early intervention/early childhood special education.

The book contains recommended practices in the following areas:

- Assessment—*John Neisworth and Stephen Bagnato*
- Child-focused interventions—*Mark Wolery*
- Family-based practices—*Carol Trivette and Carl Dunst*
- Interdisciplinary models—*R.A. McWilliam*
- Technology applications—*Kathleen Stremel*
- Policies, procedures, and systems change— *Gloria Harbin and Christine Salisbury*
- Personnel preparation—*Patricia Miller and Vicki Stayton*

DEC Recommended Practices has been completely updated with additional resources and advice, program checklists for both parents and administrators, and two new chapters dealing with the real-life experiences of users. Put *DEC Recommended Practices* to work for your students today!

G143REC

SOPRIS WEST™
EDUCATIONAL SERVICES

A Cambium Learning™ Company

Phone: (800) 547-6747
Fax: (888) 819-7767
www.sopriswest.com

Young Exceptional Children is **unique** *and*

practical*! It is designed for any adult who works*

or lives with a young child who has a disability, develop-

mental delay, special gifts or talents, or other special needs.

Young Exceptional Children (YEC) is a peer-reviewed publication produced four times per year by the Division for Early Childhood (DEC) of
the Council for Exceptional Children (CEC) with practical ideas for early
childhood teachers, therapists, parents, and administrators. Topics include:
challenging behaviors, family-guided routines, developmentally
appropriate practices for children with special needs, best practices
for young children with autism, strategies for successful inclusion, practical ideas for parents and professionals to promote
learning and development, and more!

Related Sopris West Publications

For more information about the *YEC Monograph Series* or the following resources, call **(800) 547-6747** or visit **www.sopriswest.com**

First Step to Success
Helping Young Children Overcome Antisocial Behavior

by Hill Walker, Ph.D.; Bruce Stiller, Ph.D.; Annemieke Golly, Ph.D.; Kate Kavanagh, Ph.D.; Herbert Severson, Ph.D.; and Edward Feil, Ph.D.

In collaboration with the Council for Exceptional Children

Grades K-3

This best-practices early intervention program was developed for children who either display an antisocial behavior pattern or show clear signs of developing one. By intervening early and taking a collaborative home/school approach, you can divert these children from a path that often leads to adjustment problems, school failure and dropout, delinquency, and even violence. Through the *First Step* program, children at risk can learn how to get along with teachers and peers and how to engage in schoolwork appropriately, so that they can succeed. The program utilizes three interrelated components:

- *First Step Screening*—proactive, universal screening options utilizing teacher ratings
- *First Step CLASS*—a time-tested school intervention newly adapted for young children
- *homeBase*—a family-centered, six-week intervention that enlists parents in teaching their children such school-related skills as cooperation, making friends, accepting limits, developing self-esteem, problem-solving, and sharing about school.

The **Starter Kit** contains everything you need for three implementations: *Implementation Guide, homeBase Consultant Guide,* three *homeBase Parent Handbooks, Overview Videotape,* stopwatch, three sets of *CLASS* cards, lanyard, and three *homeBase Parent Boxes* containing help cards, activity cards, timer, paper, markers, and stickers. A **Resupply Kit** contains everything needed for one additional implementation: *homeBase Parent Handbook,* one set of *CLASS* cards, and a complete *homeBase Parent Box.* Professional development is also available.

G98FIRST First Step to Success Kit

On Track
A Comprehensive System
for Early Childhood Intervention

by Shelley Neilsen, M.Ed.; Richard van den Pol, Ph.D.; Jean Guidry, Ed.S.; Elizabeth Keeley; and Rhonda Alt Honzel

Grades PreK-3

IDEA '97 entitles preschoolers with disabilities to IEPs that address the following domains:

- Physical
- Communication
- Social/Emotional
- Cognitive
- Adaptive

On Track meets this need and helps preschoolers gain the skills they need to successfully transition to school. Four components make it easier to implement and evaluate interventions:

1. The **Assessment** component includes "IEP Assessment" and "Family Interview."
2. The **Curriculum** component includes a menu of teaching programs that address skills commonly identified as important for independence, social growth, and school readiness.
3. The **Planning** component enables you to integrate specific interventions and IEP objectives into lessons.
4. The **Monitoring** component provides a well-defined structure for evaluating progress. Professional development is also available.

G66MAN

Good Talking Words
A Social Communications Skills Program

by Lucy Hart Paulson, M.S. and Rick van den Pol, Ph.D.

Grades PreK-K

Teach your students developmentally appropriate social communication skills using an active instructional approach. Twelve lessons focus on specific concepts and vocabulary to help children develop cooperative, prosocial behaviors. Students acquire specific communication skills and learn to initiate interactions and respond in socially appropriate ways. Skills such as listening, taking turns, and sharing are learned through practice, modeling, reinforcement, and reteaching. This program will enhance classroom management and reduce disruptive behaviors. Professional development is also available.

G100TALKING
Book, Set of 43 Blackline Masters, Set of 19 Skill Pictures, and 11 Posters

Please! Teach ALL of Me
Multisensory Activities for Preschoolers

by Jackie Crawford, M.S., L.P.; Marcia Gums, Ed.S.; Joni Hanson; and Paula Neys

Grades PreK-2

With this collection of hundreds of multisensory activities, you'll be able to evaluate sensory strengths and select tactile, gustatory and olfactory, auditory, and visual activities. Also includes sections on emotional development, motor skill, language, math, and cognitive development. Written by early childhood and special education, occupational therapy, speech and language therapy, and psychology professionals, this book provides a balanced, integrated approach to early childhood instruction in straightforward "teacher language." Incorporates multisensory instruction theory. Speaker Available.

G52ALL   Please! Teach ALL of Me

Teaching Kids & Adults with Autism
Building the Framework for Lifetime Learning

by Kathleen McConnell Fad, Ph.D. and L. Rozelle Moulton, M.S.

Grades PreK-Adult

Drawing from both a highly structured behavioral teaching model and multisensory communication strategies, this book provides suggestions and tools to help you develop positive communication strategies; practical behavior management techniques; and a structured teaching model for direct instruction. Using this combination, you can teach your students with autism, communication disorders, or significant developmental disabilities the requisite skills in five areas: preparation for learning; cooperation; learning by imitating and matching; independent learning; basic and higher-level communication skills.

Straightforward approaches for helping students generalize their skills, solutions to frequently encountered problems, and answers to common questions are also offered. The book includes all the necessary reproducibles. The *Materials Kit* includes signs, auditory communication aids, menu board, stopwatch, beeper tape, timer, and many more materials that will make the strategies even easier to implement. Professional development is also available.

G118BKIT Autism Book & Materials Kit
G118AUT Autism Book
G118KIT   Autism Materials Kit

To order more copies of
*Practical Ideas for Addressing
Challenging Behaviors*, contact: